A275 Reading Classical Greek: language and literature

Language Reference Book

Prepared for the module team by James Robson and Jeremy Taylor

This publication forms part of the Open University module A275 *Reading Classical Greek: language and literature*. Details of this and other Open University modules can be obtained from the Student Registration and Enquiry Service, The Open University, PO Box 197, Milton Keynes MK7 6BJ, United Kingdom (tel. +44 (0)845 300 60 90; email general-enquiries@open.ac.uk).

Alternatively, you may visit the Open University website at www.open.ac.uk where you can learn more about the wide range of modules and packs offered at all levels by The Open University.

To purchase a selection of Open University materials visit www.ouw.co.uk, or contact Open University Worldwide, Walton Hall, Milton Keynes MK7 6AA, United Kingdom for a brochure (tel. +44 (0)1908 858793; fax +44 (0)1908 858787; email ouw-customer-services@open.ac.uk).

The Open University
Walton Hall, Milton Keynes
MK7 6AA

First published 2009

Second edition 2011

Edited and designed by The Open University.

Typeset by The Open University.

Printed and bound in the United Kingdom by Charlesworth Press, Wakefield.

ISBN 978 1 8487 3947 5

2.1

B/a275_lrb_e2i1_n9781848739475

Contents

Introduction

Please read this introduction carefully before using this Language Reference Book.

The primary aim of this book is to set out in clear and legible form the tables of verbs, nouns and adjectives that you meet in *Reading Greek*. The book is also designed to provide you with extra help on some points of grammar where the explanations in *Reading Greek* are a little over-concise. It provides summaries of key grammatical concepts, and aims to answer some of the specific, more complex, questions occasionally raised by students. In addition this to, it contains a list of all the vocabulary you are asked to learn.

Some of the material in this book has been included for reference and interest purposes only, and you will therefore not need to master this information to be successful in this module.

Please take care to note:

- Grammatical forms marked with an **asterisk** (*) will ***not*** be tested in **any part** of the examination.
- Grammatical forms marked with a **dagger** (†) will ***not*** be tested in **Part 1** of the examination (the compulsory foundation-level language section). These forms may, however, be tested in **Part 2** of the examination (the optional higher-level language section) and are taken from Sections 7 to 9 of *Reading Greek.*
- Grammatical forms marked with an asterisk or a dagger may, however, be tested in the TMAs.
- When the notes specify that a point of grammar is given '**for information**' only, it will ***not*** be assessed in any part of the examination or in the TMAs.

This grammar book is intended as a resource for you to dip in and out of when you see fit, and for you to use in a number of ways as you study. As you learn the language we advise you to use the *Reading Greek* volumes and the Language Study Guide as your first port of call. You can then use this book as a point of reference in which all the tables of grammar and vocabulary relevant to your study are collected in one place. You may also wish to use this book in the following ways: to see tables of grammatical forms laid out clearly, to expand on a point of grammar you have already begun to master, or to help in your revision in the later stages of your study. However you use the book, we hope that you will find it helpful.

A note on accents. The acute (´) circumflex (˜) and grave (`) accents have been included in the tables laid out in this booklet. You are ***not***, as a rule, required to reproduce these accents in your TMA or examination answers for A275 (the exception being the rare occasion when the presence or absence of an acute accent is decisive for the sense of a word, e.g. τίς, *who*? and τις, *someone*). Please bear in mind, though, that you ***will*** be expected to reproduce the rough breathing (῾) and smooth breathing (᾿) and iota subscript (ͺ).

Finally, the decision has been taken not to provide 'meanings' for most of the verb forms listed in the tables in this book. This is for the sake of space, practicality, and to discourage the notion that there is one 'right' way of translating a given verb form.

1 Letters and sounds

The alphabet

The following table provides a pronunciation guide for each letter of the Greek alphabet, along with examples of words starting with that letter. (Note that some of the pronunciations suggested here differ slightly from those recommended in *Reading Greek*.)

Letter	Name	Vowel or consonant	Sound	Example words
Α α	alpha	v.	**a** as in 'c**a**p' or 'r**a**ther'	ἀκούω, *I hear*; ἄνθρωπος, *man*
Β β	beta	c.	**b**	βαίνω, *I go*; βάρβαρος, *barbarian*
Γ γ	gamma	c.	**g** as in '**g**et'	γεωργός, *farmer*; γῆ, *land*
Δ δ	delta	c.	**d**	δεσπότης, *master*; δεῦρο, *here*
Ε ε	epsilon	v.	short **e** as in 'j**e**t'	ἐλεύθερος, *free*; ἐν, *in*
Ζ ζ	zeta	c.	**z** as in '**z**ebra'; **sd** as in 'wi**sd**om'	Ζεύς, *Zeus*; ζητέω, *I look for*
Η η	eta	v.	**ē** as in '**air**' or 'p**ear**'	ἤδη, *already*; ἡδέως, *sweetly*
Θ θ	theta	c.	**th** as in '**th**in'	θάλαττα, *sea*; θεά, *goddess*
Ι ι	iota	v.	**i** as in '**sin**' or '**seed**'	ἴσως, *perhaps*; ἵππος, *horse*
Κ κ	kappa	c.	**k**	καί, *and*; καλός, *beautiful*
Λ λ	lambda	c.	**l**	λέγω, *I say*; λόγος, *story*
Μ μ	mu	c.	**m**	μένω, *I wait*; μῶρος, *stupid*
Ν ν	nu	c.	**n**	ναί, *yes*; ναύτης, *sailor*
Ξ ξ	xi	c.	**x** as in 'bo**x**'	ξένος, *foreigner*; ξύλον, *wood*
Ο ο	omicron	v.	**o** as in 'b**o**x'	ὀρθός, *straight*; ὁράω, *I see*
Π π	pi	c.	**p**	περί, *about*; ποιέω, *I make, do*
Ρ ρ	rho	c.	**r**	ῥίπτω, *I throw*; ῥᾴδιος, *easy*
Σ σ ς[1]	sigma	c.	**s**	σαφῶς, *clearly*; σῶος, *safe*
Τ τ	tau	c.	**t**	τέχνη, *skill*; τίς, *who*?
Υ υ	upsilon	v.	**oo** as in 'sh**oe**' (or, better, as in French 'l**u**ne' or German 'M**ü**ller')	ὕβρις, *aggression*; ὑμεῖς, *you* (pl.)
Φ φ	phi	c.	**ph**/**f** as in '**f**eel'	φεύγω, *I flee*; φίλος, *friend*
Χ χ	khi	c.	**kh** as in 'lo**ch**'	χωρέω, *I go*; χρηστός, *fine*
Ψ ψ	psi	c.	**ps**	ψευδῶς, *falsely*; ψυχή, *soul*
Ω ω	omega	v.	long **o** as in 'b**ough**t'	ὤν, *being*; ὥσπερ, *like*

[1] σ and ς are distinguished by their position in a word. If the letter comes at the beginning or within a word, σ form is used; if it comes at the end of a word, ς is used – e.g. στάσις.

Diphthongs

A diphthong is a combination of two vowels pronounced as one sound (like the letters 'ou' in the word 'pronounced'). The Greek diphthongs are set out below.

Diphthong	Sound	Example words
αι	as in 'high'	αἰτία, *reason*; βαίνω, *I go*
αυ	as in 'now'	αὖθις, *again*; ναύτης, *sailor*
ει	as in 'fiancée'	εἰς, *into*; ὑμεῖς, *you* (pl.)
ευ	(pronounce both elements separately, starting with 'e', as in 'bed', and ending with 'ou', as in 'should')	εὐχή, *prayer*; δεῦρο, *here*
οι	as in 'boy'	οἶδα, *I know*; ποιέω, *I make, do*
ου	as in 'too'	οὐδέν, *nothing*; ἀκούω, *I hear*

Consonantal combinations with γ (gamma)

γ combines with γ, κ, ξ and χ to produce an 'n' sound.

γ + consonant	Sound
γγ	'ng' as in ἄγγελος, angelos, *messenger* (pronounced like 'ng' in a**ng**er)
γκ	'nk' as in ἄγκυρα, ankura, *anchor*
γξ	'nx' as in σφίγξ, sphinx

Iota subscript

Iota (ι) after a lower case η (eta) or ω (omega) is written underneath the letter – ῃ, ῳ. It is also written thus if it follows a long α (alpha) – ᾳ (i.e. when alpha is pronounced like the 'a' in 'f**a**ther' rather than 'c**a**p'). This represents the trace of an original iota sound attached to some words, which eventually became so weak that it was retained only in the spelling; for example:

ἐν τῇ γῇ, *on the land*

λέγω τῷ ἀνθρώπῳ, *I speak to the man*

ὁρᾷ, *he sees.*

Breathings

Every word beginning with a vowel (α, ε, η, ι, ο, υ, ω) or a rho (ρ) has a mark above it called a 'breathing'. A 'rough' breathing (῾) indicates that the word is pronounced with an initial 'h' sound, whereas a 'smooth' breathing (᾿) indicates the absence of an 'h' sound. Thus:

ἡδέως, *sweetly*

ὁράω, *I see*;

cf. ἤδη, *already*

ὄνομα, *name*.

When the initial letter is a capital, the breathing appears to the left of the letter rather than above it:

Ἀθῆναι, *Athens*

Ἕλλην, *Greek*.

If a word starts with a diphthong (i.e. two vowels pronounced as one sound), the breathing appears above the second letter:

οἰκία, *house*

αἱρέω, *take, capture*.

Note that words beginning with upsilon (υ) or rho (ρ) always take a rough breathing:

ῥᾴδιος, *easy*

ὕβρις, *violence*.

Punctuation

Greek is punctuated using full stops and commas, as in English. An English semicolon (;) is the sign for a question mark (?), and a raised dot (·) is used as a colon (:) or semicolon (;).

Accents

You do not need to write the three accents of ancient Greek: the acute (´), grave (`) and circumflex (~). They were invented in antiquity to help readers pronounce every Greek word with the correct musical 'pitch' (i.e. with a rising or falling tone). The acute accent marks a rising tone, the circumflex a rising and falling tone, and the grave either a falling or a neutral tone. As English is pronounced with stress rather than pitch, accents are difficult for English speakers to use as intended, and are mostly of interest to specialists. Nevertheless, as almost all ancient Greek is printed with accents (including the Greek in *Reading Greek*), it is worth becoming familiar with their appearance, even if you do not make use of them.

2 Word shape

The definite article

ὁ, ἡ, τό, *the*

sing.

	masc.	**fem.**	**neut.**
nom.	ὁ	ἡ	τό
acc.	τόν	τήν	τό
gen.	τοῦ	τῆς	τοῦ
dat.	τῷ	τῇ	τῷ

pl.

	masc.	**fem.**	**neut.**
nom.	οἱ	αἱ	τά
acc.	τούς	τάς	τά
gen.	τῶν	τῶν	τῶν
dat.	τοῖς	ταῖς	τοῖς

Note 1 ὅδε, ἥδε, τόδε, *this*, follows the same pattern of declension.

Nouns

1st declension nouns

ἡ βοή (1a), *shout*

	sing.	pl.
nom.	βο-ή	βο-αί
acc.	βο-ήν	βο-άς
gen.	βο-ῆς	βο-ῶν
dat.	βο-ῇ	βο-αῖς

ἡ ἀπορία (1b), *perplexity*

	sing.	pl.
nom.	ἀπορί-α	ἀπορί-αι
acc.	ἀπορί-αν	ἀπορί-ας
gen.	ἀπορί-ας	ἀπορι-ῶν
dat.	ἀπορί-ᾳ	ἀπορί-αις

ἡ θάλαττα, (1c), *sea*

	sing.	pl.
nom.	θάλαττ-α	θάλαττ-αι
acc.	θάλαττ-αν	θαλάττ-ας
gen.	θαλάττ-ης	θαλαττ-ῶν
dat.	θαλάττ-ῃ	θαλάττ-αις

ὁ ναύτης (1d), *sailor*

	sing.	pl.
nom.	ναύτ-ης	ναῦτ-αι
acc.	ναύτ-ην	ναύτ-ας
gen.	ναύτ-ου	ναυτ-ῶν
dat.	ναύτ-ῃ	ναύτ-αις

ὁ νεανίας (1d), *young man*

	sing.	pl.
nom.	νεανί-ας	νεανί-αι
acc.	νεανί-αν	νεανί-ας
gen.	νεανί-ου	νεανι-ῶν
dat.	νεανί-ᾳ	νεανί-αις

Note 1 All type 1a, 1b and 1c nouns are feminine; all type 1d nouns are masculine.

Note 2 All 1st declension nouns are declined in the same way in the plural.

Note 3 Distinguish between type 1b and 1c nouns, both of whose nominative singular forms end in -α. Type 1b noun stems end in ε, ι or ρ; thus: ἡ θεά (1b), *goddess*; ἡ οἰκία (1b), *house*; ἡ πυρά*, (1b), *funeral pyre*, *fire signal*. Unlike type 1c nouns, they add -ας to their stem to form the genitive singular and -ᾳ to form the dative singular.

Note 4 NB the genitive singular of type 1d nouns (-ου).

Note 5 Type 1d nouns are generally 'agent' nouns and so are often job titles: ὁ κυβερνήτης* (1d), *captain*; ὁ ποιητής (1d), *poet*; ὁ οἰκέτης* (1d), *house-slave*.

Note also ὁ κλέπτης† (1d), *thief*; ὁ θεατής† (1d), *spectator*; ὁ ἱκέτης* (1d), *suppliant*. νεανίας is the only 1d noun you meet ending in -ας.

2nd declension nouns

ὁ ἄνθρωπος (2a), *man*

	sing.	pl.
nom.	ἄνθρωπ-ος	ἄνθρωπ-οι
acc.	ἄνθρωπ-ον	ἀνθρώπ-ους
gen.	ἀνθρώπ-ου	ἀνθρώπ-ων
dat.	ἀνθρώπ-ῳ	ἀνθρώπ-οις

Note 1 The vast majority of type 2a nouns are masculine. A small group, however, are feminine. The two examples of feminine 2a nouns that you meet are given in the tables below. Please note that while these nouns decline no differently from their masculine counterparts, they must, of course, where appropriate, be preceded by the feminine definite article.

ἡ νῆσος (2a), *island*

	sing.	pl.
nom.	νῆσ-ος	νῆσ-οι
acc.	νῆσ-ον	νήσ-ους
gen.	νήσ-ου	νήσ-ων
dat.	νήσ-ῳ	νήσ-οις

ἡ νόσος (2a), *illness, plague*

	sing.	pl.
nom.	νόσ-ος	νόσ-οι
acc.	νόσ-ον	νόσ-ους
gen.	νόσ-ου	νόσ-ων
dat.	νόσ-ῳ	νόσ-οις

Note 2 You also meet the noun θεός, which means 'god' when masculine and 'goddess' when feminine.

For information: the noun ὁ νοῦς, *mind* (a contraction of νό-ος) declines in the following way. You will not be asked to reproduce forms of this noun in your assessed work or in the examination.

ὁ νοῦς* (2a), *mind*

	sing.	pl.
nom.	νοῦς	νοῖ
acc.	νοῦν	νοῦς
gen.	νοῦ	νῶν
dat.	νῷ	νοῖς

τὸ ἔργον (2b), *task, deed*

	sing.	pl.
nom.	ἔργ-ον	ἔργ-α
acc.	ἔργ-ον	ἔργ-α
gen.	ἔργ-ου	ἔργ-ων
dat.	ἔργ-ῳ	ἔργ-οις

Note 1 All type 2b nouns are neuter. Both in the singular and plural the endings of neuter nouns are always the same in the nominative and accusative.

3rd declension nouns

ὁ λιμήν (λιμεν-) (3a), *harbour*

	sing.	**pl.**
nom.	λιμήν	λιμέν-ες
acc.	λιμέν-α	λιμέν-ας
gen.	λιμέν-ος	λιμέν-ων
dat.	λιμέν-ι	λιμέσι (ν)

ἡ νύξ (νυκτ-) (3a), *night*

	sing.	**pl.**
nom.	νύξ	νύκτ-ες
acc.	νύκτ-α	νύκτ-ας
gen.	νυκτ-ός	νυκτ-ῶν
dat.	νυκτ-ί	νυξί(ν)

Note 1 Type 3a nouns may be either masculine, like λιμήν, or feminine, like νύξ: the gender of each noun must be learnt when met. The dative plural results from a combination of the stem plus the ending σι; e.g. λιμέν-σι: λιμέσι. The ways in which the stem and ending combine are laid out in Appendix Two of this book.

ὁ πατήρ (πατ(ε)ρ-) (3a), *father*

	sing.	**pl.**
nom.	πατήρ	πατέρ-ες
acc.	πατέρ-α	πατέρ-ας
gen.	πατρ-ός	πατέρ-ων
dat.	πατρ-ί	πατράσι(ν)

Note 1 πατήρ is exceptional amongst the nouns that you meet, in that its stem is syncopated (i.e. a syllable drops out) in the genitive and dative singular and in the dative plural: it is πατρ- rather than πατερ-. It is for this reason that the noun is laid out here.

Note 2 **For information**: πατήρ is a member of the so-called ‘family group’. ἡ μήτηρ (μητ(ε)ρ-), *mother* and ἡ θυγάτηρ (θυγατ(ε)ρ-), *daughter* behave in the same way – as does ἡ γαστήρ (γαστ(ε)ρ-), *stomach*.

τὸ πρᾶγμα (πραγματ-) (3b), *thing, matter*

	sing.	pl.
nom.	πρᾶγμα	πράγματ-α
acc.	πρᾶγμα	πράγματ-α
gen.	πράγματ-ος	πραγμάτ-ων
dat.	πράγματ-ι	πράγμασι(ν)

Other 3b nouns met are: τὸ δρᾶμα† (δραματ-), *play, drama*; τὸ κτῆμα† (κτηματ-), *possession*; τὸ ὄνομα† (ὀνοματ-), *name*; τὸ πῦρ† (πυρ-), *fire*.

Note 1 All type 3b nouns are neuter.

Note 2 Be careful not to confuse 3b nouns with 1c nouns like ἡ θάλαττα, *sea*.

τὸ πλῆθος (3c), *number, crowd, the people*

	sing.	pl.
nom.	πλῆθ-ος	πλήθ-η
acc.	πλῆθ-ος	πλήθ-η
gen.	πλήθ-ους	πληθ-ῶν
dat.	πλήθε-ι	πλήθεσι(ν)

Other 3c nouns met are: τὸ μέρος†, *part, share*; τὸ πάθος†, *suffering, experience*; τὰ σκεύη (pl.), *gear, furniture*.

Note 1 All type 3c nouns are neuter.

Note 2 Do not confuse type 3c nouns with type 2a nouns such as ὁ ἄνθρωπος, *man*.

ἡ τριήρης* (3d), *trireme*

	sing.	pl.
nom.	τριήρ-ης	τριήρ-εις
acc.	τριήρ-η	τριήρ-εις
gen.	τριήρ-ους	τριήρ-ων
dat.	τριήρ-ει	τριήρεσι(ν)

Other 3d nouns met are: ὁ συγγενής†, *relation*; ὁ Σωκράτης*, *Socrates*.

Note 1 Type 3d nouns may be masculine or feminine: the gender of each noun must be learnt when met.

Note 2 Do not confuse type 3d nouns with type 1d nouns such as ὁ ναύτης, *sailor*.

ὁ Περικλῆς* (3d uncontracted), *Pericles*

	sing.	pl.
nom.	Περικλῆς	no plural
acc.	Περικλέα	no plural
gen.	Περικλέους	no plural
dat.	Περικλεῖ	no plural

The other 3d (uncontracted) noun met is: ὁ Ἡρακλῆς*, *Heracles*.

ἡ πόλις (3e), *city-state*

	sing.	pl.
nom.	πόλι-ς	πόλεις
acc.	πόλι-ν	πόλεις
gen.	πόλε-ως	πόλε-ων
dat.	πόλε-ι	πόλεσι(ν)

Other 3e -ις nouns met are: ἡ οἴκησις, *dwelling*; ἡ τάξις*, *order, rank, battle array*; ἡ ὕβρις, *aggression, violence, insult, humiliation*.

Note 1 All 3e nouns ending in -ις in the nominative singular are feminine.

ὁ πρέσβυς (3e), *old man;* pl. *ambassadors*

	sing.	pl.
nom.	πρέσβυ-ς	πρέσβεις
acc.	πρέσβυ-ν	πρέσβεις
gen.	πρέσβε-ως	πρέσβ εων
dat.	πρέσβε-ι	πρέσβεσι(ν)

ὁ πρέσβυς is the only 3e -υς noun met.

τὸ ἄστυ (3f), *city*

	sing.	pl.
nom.	ἄστυ	ἄστ-η
acc.	ἄστυ	ἄστ-η
gen.	ἄστ-εως	ἄστ-εων
dat.	ἄστ-ει	ἄστεσι(ν)

τὸ ἄστυ is the only 3f noun met.

ὁ βασιλεύς (3g), *king*

	sing.	pl.
nom.	βασιλεύ-ς	βασιλῆς (or βασιλ-εῖς*)
acc.	βασιλέ-α	βασιλέ-ας
gen.	βασιλέ-ως	βασιλέ-ων
dat.	βασιλε-ῖ	βασιλεῦσι(ν)

ὁ βασιλεύς is the only 3g noun met.

ἡ ὀφρῦς† (3h), *eyebrow*

	sing.	pl.
nom.	ὀφρύ-ς	ὀφρύ-ες
acc.	ὀφρύ-ν	ὀφρῦ-ς
gen.	ὀφρύ-ος	ὀφρύ-ων
dat.	ὀφρύ-ι	ὀφρύσι(ν)

ἡ ὀφρῦς is the only 3h noun met.

Irregular nouns

ἡ ναῦς, *ship*

	sing.	**pl.**
nom.	ναῦς	νῆες
acc.	ναῦν	ναῦς
gen.	νεώς	νεῶν
dat.	νηί	ναυσί(ν)

ὁ Ζεύς, *Zeus*

	sing.	**pl.**
nom.	Ζεύς	no plural
acc.	Δί-α	no plural
gen.	Δι-ός	no plural
dat.	Δι-ί	no plural

Note 1 The endings of ὁ Ζεύς are the same as for regular type 3a nouns. It is classed as irregular because of the unusual change in its stem.

*Vocative forms of nouns**

The vocative is the case used when a person or thing is directly addressed (as in 'grandmother' in 'O grandmother, what big teeth you have!'). The vocative form of nouns is often the same as the nominative in the singular and always the same as the nominative in the plural. Those noun types which display different nominative and vocative singulars are as follows.

1d	ναῦτα νεανία
2a	ἄνθρωπε
3d	τριῆρες Περίκλεις
3e	πόλι
3g	βασιλεῦ
3h	ὀφρύ

The vocatives of type 3a nouns are less easy to predict, although they are easily recognisable. Here are some examples.

ὁ ἀνήρ (ἀνδρ-) ἄνερ, *man*

ὁ δαίμων (δαιμον-) δαῖμον, *god*

ὁ Ἕλλην (Ἑλλην-) Ἕλλην, *Greek*

ἡ νύξ (νυκτ-) νύξ, *night*

ὁ πατήρ (πατ(ε)ρ-) πάτερ, *father*

ὁ σωτήρ (σωτηρ-) σῶτερ, *saviour*

Adjectives

Type 1/2 adjectives

You will sometimes find these described as '212' adjectives, since their declension follows that of type 2 masculine, type 1 feminine and type 2 neuter nouns.

καλ-ός ή όν, *beautiful, fine*

sing.

	masc.	**fem.**	**neut.**
nom.	καλ-ός	καλ-ή	καλ-όν
acc.	καλ-όν	καλ-ήν	καλ-όν
gen.	καλ-οῦ	καλ-ῆς	καλ-οῦ
dat.	καλ-ῷ	καλ-ῇ	καλ-ῷ

pl.

	masc.	**fem.**	**neut.**
nom.	καλ-οί	καλ-αί	καλ-ά
acc.	καλ-ούς	καλ-άς	καλ-ά
gen.	καλ-ῶν	καλ-ῶν	καλ-ῶν
dat.	καλ-οῖς	καλ-αῖς	καλ-οῖς

ἡμέτερ-ος α ον, *our*

sing.

	masc.	**fem.**	**neut.**
nom.	ἡμέτερ-ος	ἡμετέρ-α	ἡμέτερ-ον
acc.	ἡμέτερ-ον	ἡμετέρ-αν	ἡμέτερ-ον
gen.	ἡμετέρ-ου	ἡμετέρ-ας	ἡμετέρ-ου
dat.	ἡμετέρ-ῳ	ἡμετέρ-ᾳ	ἡμετέρ-ῳ

pl.

	masc.	**fem.**	**neut.**
nom.	ἡμέτερ-οι	ἡμέτερ-αι	ἡμέτερ-α
acc.	ἡμετέρ-ους	ἡμετέρ-ας	ἡμέτερ-α
gen.	ἡμετέρ-ων	ἡμετέρ-ων	ἡμετέρ-ων
dat.	ἡμετέρ-οις	ἡμετέρ-αις	ἡμετέρ-οις

Note 1 Adjectives of the ἡμέτερ-ος α ον type may be easily identified since their stems end in ε, ι or ρ. Thus νέ-ος α ον, *young*; ἀνδρεῖ-ος α ον†, *brave*; πολέμι-ος α ον, *hostile*; and μῶρ-ος α ον, *stupid*. σῶ-ος α ον, *safe*, declines in the same way, with α rather than η in all cases of the feminine singular.

Type 3 adjectives

You will sometimes find these described as '333' adjectives, since their declension follows that of type 3a masculine/feminine and type 3b neuter nouns.

εὔφρων, εὖφρον (εὐφρον-), *well-disposed*

sing.

	masc./fem.	**neut.**
nom.	εὔφρων	εὖφρον
acc.	εὔφρον-α	εὖφρον
gen.	εὔφρον-ος	εὔφρον-ος
dat.	εὔφρον-ι	εὔφρον-ι

pl.

	masc./fem.	**neut.**
nom.	εὔφρον-ες	εὔφρον-α
acc.	εὔφρον-ας	εὔφρον-α
gen.	εὐφρόν-ων	εὐφρόν-ων
dat.	εὔφροσι(ν)	εὔφροσι(ν)

βελτίων, βέλτιον (βελτιον-), *better* (comparative of ἀγαθός)†

sing.

	masc./fem.	**neut.**
nom.	βελτίων	βέλτιον
acc.	βελτίον-α or βελτίω*	βέλτιον
gen.	βελτίον-ος	βελτίον-ος
dat.	βελτίον-ι	βελτίον-ι

pl.

	masc./fem.	**neut.**
nom.	βελτίον-ες or βελτίους*	βελτίον-α or βελτίω*
acc.	βελτίον-ας or βελτίους*	βελτίον-α or βελτίω*
gen.	βελτιόν-ων	βελτιόν-ων
dat.	βελτίοσι(ν)	βελτίοσι(ν)

Note 1 The alternative forms are found in relation to comparative adjectives and do *not* apply to other type 3 adjectives. The alternative forms need not be learnt for the examination.

Other adjectives

πολύς, πολλή, πολύ (πολλ-), ***much, many***

sing.

	masc.	**fem.**	**neut.**
nom.	πολύς	πολλ-ή	πολύ
acc.	πολύν	πολλ-ήν	πολύ
gen.	πολλ-οῦ	πολλ-ῆς	πολλ-οῦ
dat.	πολλ-ῷ	πολλ-ῇ	πολλ-ῷ

pl.

	masc.	**fem.**	**neut.**
nom.	πολλ-οί	πολλ-αί	πολλ-ά
acc.	πολλ-ούς	πολλ-άς	πολλ-ά
gen.	πολλ-ῶν	πολλ-ῶν	πολλ-ῶν
dat.	πολλ-οῖς	πολλ-αῖς	πολλ-οῖς

Note 1 Apart from the masculine and neuter nominative and accusative singular forms, this adjective declines like an adjective of the καλ-ός ή όν type, with stem πολλ-.

μέγας, μεγάλη, μέγα (μεγαλ-), ***big, great***

sing.

	masc.	**fem.**	**neut.**
nom.	μέγας	μεγάλ-η	μέγα
acc.	μέγαν	μεγάλ-ην	μέγα
gen.	μεγάλ-ου	μεγάλ-ης	μεγάλ-ου
dat.	μεγάλ-ῳ	μεγάλ-ῃ	μεγάλ-ῳ

pl.

	masc.	**fem.**	**neut.**
nom.	μεγάλ-οι	μεγάλ-αι	μεγάλ-α
acc.	μεγάλ-ους	μεγάλ-ας	μεγάλ-α
gen.	μεγάλ-ων	μεγάλ-ων	μεγάλ-ων
dat.	μεγάλ-οις	μεγάλ-αις	μεγάλ-οις

Note 1 Like πολύς, πολλή, πολύ, apart from the masculine and neuter nominative and accusative singular forms, this adjective declines like an adjective of the καλ-ός ή όν type, with stem μεγαλ-.

πᾶς, πᾶσα, πᾶν, (παντ-), ***all (whole)*** †

sing.

	masc.	**fem.**	**neut.**
nom.	πᾶς	πᾶσ-α	πᾶν
acc.	πάντ-α	πᾶσ-αν	πᾶν
gen.	παντ-ός	πάσ-ης	παντ-ός
dat.	παντ-ί	πάσ-ῃ	παντ-ί

pl.

	masc.	**fem.**	**neut.**
nom.	πάντ-ες	πᾶσ-αι	πάντ-α
acc.	πάντ-ας	πάσ-ας	πάντ-α
gen.	πάντ-ων	πασ-ῶν	πάντ-ων
dat.	πᾶσι(ν)	πάσ-αις	πᾶσι(ν)

Note 1 In its masculine forms this adjective changes like 3a nouns, in its feminine forms like type 1c nouns, and in the neuter like type 3b nouns. This is an important adjective type as the same pattern of declension is found in both present and aorist participles. μέλας, μέλαινα, μέλαν†, *black*, and τάλας, τάλαινα, τάλαν†, *wretched*, *unhappy*, decline in the same way.

*Further adjective types**

For information: a handful of the adjectives you meet in Sections 1–9 of *G&E* do not follow these patterns of declension.

ἄγροικ-ος ον, *from the country, boorish*
ἄδικ-ος ον, *unjust*
ἀδύνατ-ος ον, *impossible*
ἔμπειρ-ος ον, *skilled, experienced*

These are ‘two-termination’ adjectives; i.e. there are no distinct feminine forms. **For information** on these, see *G&E*, p. 230 §226.

Two further adjective types, γλυκύς, γλυκεῖα, γλυκύ, *sweet*, and ἀμελής, ἀμελές, *uncaring*, are dealt with in *G&E*, pp. 214–15 §215. In *G&E* Sections 1–9, you meet ἡδύς, ἡδεῖα, ἡδύ, *sweet, pleasant*, which changes like γλυκύς, and ἀμαθής, ἀμαθές, *ignorant*, which changes like ἀμελής.

πλέως, πλέα, πλέων, *full*, also has a distinctive declension: it is a contract adjective, not set out in *G&E*.

You will not be asked to reproduce forms of these adjectives either in your assessed work or in the examination.

*Vocative forms of adjectives**

Vocative forms of adjectives are the same as the nominative except, occasionally, in the masculine singular. Of the adjective types you have learnt, the following have distinct masculine singular vocative forms:

καλ-ός η ον	→	καλέ
ἡμέτερ-ος α ον	→	ἡμέτερε
εὔφρων ον	→	εὖφρον

Comparative and superlative adjectives†

Regular formation: type 1/2 adjectives

positive	**comparative**	**superlative**
σοφ-ός, *wise*	σοφ-ώτερ-ος α ον, *wiser*	σοφ-ώτατ-ος η ον, *wisest*
δειν-ός, *terrible*	δειν-ότερ-ος α ον, *more terrible*	δειν-ότατ-ος η ον, *most terrible*

Note 1 When the last syllable of the adjective's stem is short (i.e. contains a single short vowel as in σοφ-ός), -ώτερος and -ώτατος are added to form the comparative and superlative adjectives; when this syllable is long (i.e. contains a diphthong (double vowel), as in δειν-ός, or a long vowel, as in δῆλ-ος), -ότερος, -ότατος are added. (There are a small number of exceptions to this rule, but these need not be learnt.)

Regular formation: type 3 adjectives

positive	**comparative**	**superlative**
εὔφρων (εὐφρον-), *well-disposed*	εὐφρον-έστερ-ος α ον, *more well-disposed*	εὐφρον-έστατ-ος η ον, *most well-disposed*

Note 1 Type 3 adjectives add -εστερος and -εστατος to the stem to form the comparative and superlative adjectives.

Note 2 All regular comparative adjectives (whatever type of adjectives they are in their 'positive' form) decline in the same way as ἡμέτερ-ος α ον, and all superlative adjectives decline like καλ-ός ή όν.

Note 3 See *G&E*, p. 137 §157 for alternative translations of comparative and superlative adjectives.

Irregular formation of adjectives†

positive	comparative	superlative
ἀγαθός, *good*	ἀμείνων, ἄμεινον (ἀμεινον-) or βελτίων, βέλτιον (βελτιον-), *better*	ἄριστ-ος η ον or βέλτιστ-ος η ον, *best*
κακός, *bad*	κακίων, κάκιον (κακιον-) or χείρων, χεῖρον (χειρον-), *worse*	κάκιστ-ος η ον or χείριστ-ος η ον, *worst*
καλός, *beautiful, fine*	καλλίων, κάλλιον (καλλιον-), *more beautiful, finer*	κάλλιστ-ος η ον, *most beautiful, finest*
μέγας, *big*	μείζων, μεῖζον (μειζον-), *bigger*	μέγιστ-ος η ον, *biggest*
ὀλίγος, *small, little (few)*	ἐλάττων, ἔλαττον (ἐλαττον-)*, *less, fewer*	ἐλάχιστ-ος η ον*, *least, fewest*
πολύς, *much*	πλείων, πλεῖον (πλειον-), *more*	πλεῖστ-ος η ον, *most*
ῥᾴδιος, *easy*	ῥᾴων, ῥᾷον (ῥαον-)*, *easier*	ῥᾷστ-ος η ον*, *easiest*

Note 1 For the declension of irregular comparative adjectives, see p. 22 above. Please note that the stem of irregular comparatives ends in ν (and not ντ).

Note 2 Like regular superlative adjectives, irregular superlatives also decline like καλ-ός ή όν.

Note 3 You also meet the comparatives κρείττων, κρεῖττον (κρειττον-)†, *stronger, greater* (used as a comparative of ἀγαθός-ή όν) and ἥττων, ἧττον (ἡττον-)†, *lesser, weaker* (a comparative of ὀλίγ-ος η ον, *few*).

Adjectives/Pronouns

Indefinite adjective/pronoun

τις, τι (τιν-)
as adjective: *a, a certain* (in plural: *some*)
as pronoun: *someone, something, anyone, anything*

sing.

	masc./fem.	neut.
nom.	τις	τι
acc.	τιν-ά	τι
gen.	τιν-ός	τιν-ός
dat.	τιν-ί	τιν-ί

pl.

	masc./fem.	neut.
nom.	τιν-ές	τιν-ά
acc.	τιν-άς	τιν-ά
gen.	τιν-ῶν	τιν-ῶν
dat.	τισί(ν)	τισί(ν)

Note 1 As adjective: δοῦλός τις, *a (certain) slave*; πλοῖόν τι, *a (certain) ship*.
As pronoun: ἀφικνεῖταί τις, *someone is arriving*; ὁρᾷς τι; *do you see anything?* (*can you see anything?*)

Interrogative adjective/pronoun

τίς, τί (τίν-)
as adjective: *which? what?*
as pronoun: *who? what?*

sing.

	masc./fem.	neut.
nom.	τίς	τί
acc.	τίν-α	τί
gen.	τίν-ος	τίν-ος
dat.	τίν-ι	τίν-ι

pl.

	masc./fem.	neut.
nom.	τίν-ες	τίν-α
acc.	τίν-ας	τίν-α
gen.	τίν-ων	τίν-ων
dat.	τίσι(ν)	τίσι(ν)

Note 1 As adjective: τίς δοῦλος, *what slave?*; τί πλοῖον, *what ship?*
As pronoun: τίς ἀφικνεῖται, *who is arriving?*; τί ὁρᾷς, *what do you see? (what can you see?)*

Note 2 The accentual difference means that a classical Athenian would have *heard* the difference in sense between τις, τι and τίς, τί. Interrogative τίς, τί has an acute accent on the ι of the first syllable; indefinite τις, τι never does. There are a number of words in Greek distinguishable only by their accents, such as οὐκοῦν, *therefore*, and οὔκουν, *not ... therefore*.

Negative adjective/pronoun

οὐδείς, οὐδεμί-α, οὐδέν (οὐδεν-)
as adjective: *no*
as pronoun: *no one, nothing* (no plural)

	masc.	**fem.**	**neut.**
nom.	οὐδείς	οὐδεμί-α	οὐδέν
acc.	οὐδέν-α	οὐδεμί-αν	οὐδέν
gen.	οὐδεν-ός	οὐδεμι-ᾶς	οὐδεν-ός
dat.	οὐδεν-ί	οὐδεμι-ᾷ	οὐδεν-ί

Note 1 As adjective: οὐδεὶς δοῦλος πάρεστιν, *no slave is here*; οὐδὲν πλοῖον ὁρῶ, *I see no ship.*
As pronoun: οὐδεὶς πάρεστιν, *no one is here*; οὐδὲν ὁρῶ, *I see nothing*.

Note 2 See *G&E*, p. 64 §75 for the use of οὐδείς, οὐδεμία, οὐδέν with a negative:
οὐ μάχεται οὐδείς, *no one is fighting*
compared with
οὐδεὶς οὐ μάχεται, *everybody is fighting (no one is not fighting)*.

Demonstrative adjective/pronoun

οὗτος, αὕτη, τοῦτο
as adjective: *this*
as pronoun: *this man/woman/thing; he/she/it*

sing.

	masc.	**fem.**	**neut.**
nom.	οὗτ-ος	αὕτ-η	τοῦτ-ο
acc.	τοῦτ-ον	ταύτ-ην	τοῦτ-ο
gen.	τούτ-ου	ταύτ-ης	τούτ-ου
dat.	τούτ-ῳ	ταύτ-ῃ	τούτ-ῳ

pl.

	masc.	**fem.**	**neut.**
nom.	οὗτ-οι	αὗτ-αι	ταῦτ-α
acc.	τούτ-ους	ταύτ-ας	ταῦτ-α
gen.	τούτ-ων	τούτ-ων	τούτ-ων
dat.	τούτ-οις	ταύτ-αις	τούτ-οις

Note 1 As with the definite article, all forms except the nominative masculine and feminine singular and plural begin with τ-. τοιοῦτος, τοιαύτη, τοιοῦτο†, *of such a kind*, follows a similar pattern of declension.

Note 2 NB the spelling of the feminine genitive plural: τούτ-ων.

ἐκεῖνος, ἐκείνη, ἐκεῖνο
as adjective: *that*
as pronoun: *that man/woman/thing, he/she/it*

sing.

	masc.	**fem.**	**neut.**
nom.	ἐκεῖν-ος	ἐκείν-η	ἐκεῖν-ο
acc.	ἐκεῖν-ον	ἐκείν-ην	ἐκεῖν-ο
gen.	ἐκείν-ου	ἐκείν-ης	ἐκείν-ου
dat.	ἐκείν-ῳ	ἐκείν-ῃ	ἐκείν-ῳ

pl.

	masc.	**fem.**	**neut.**
nom.	ἐκεῖν-οι	ἐκεῖν-αι	ἐκεῖν-α
acc.	ἐκείν-ους	ἐκείν-ας	ἐκεῖν-α
gen.	ἐκείν-ων	ἐκείν-ων	ἐκείν-ων
dat.	ἐκείν-οις	ἐκείν-αις	ἐκείν-οις

Note 1 αὐτός, αὐτή, αὐτό, *same, self*, and ἄλλος, ἄλλη, ἄλλο, *other*, follow the same pattern of declension.

Pronouns

Personal pronouns

ἐγω, *I/me*

nom.	ἐγώ
acc.	με or ἐμέ
gen.	μου or ἐμοῦ
dat.	μοι or ἐμοί

Note 1 ἐμέ, ἐμοῦ, ἐμοί are emphatic forms; με, μου, μοι are unemphatic.

σύ, *you* (sing.)

nom.	σύ
acc.	σέ
gen.	σοῦ
dat.	σοί

ἡμεῖς, *we/us*

nom.	ἡμεῖς
acc.	ἡμᾶς
gen.	ἡμῶν
dat.	ἡμῖν

ὑμεῖς, *you* (pl.)

nom.	ὑμεῖς
acc.	ὑμᾶς
gen.	ὑμῶν
dat.	ὑμῖν

αὐτόν, αὐτήν, αὐτό,† *him, her, it*

	masc.	**fem.**	**neut.**
nom.	–	–	–
acc.	αὐτόν	αὐτήν	αὐτό
gen.	αὐτοῦ	αὐτῆς	αὐτοῦ
dat.	αὐτῷ	αὐτῇ	αὐτῷ

αὐτούς, αὐτάς, αὐτά,† *them*

	masc.	**fem.**	**neut.**
nom.	–	–	–
acc.	αὐτούς	αὐτάς	αὐτά
gen.	αὐτῶν	αὐτῶν	αὐτῶν
dat.	αὐτοῖς	αὐταῖς	αὐτοῖς

Note 1 Forms of οὗτος and ἐκεῖνος are also often best translated as *him/her/it/them* and are found at least as often as αὐτόν, αὐτήν, αὐτό, etc.

Reflexive pronouns†

ἐμαυτόν, ἐμαυτήν, *myself*

	masc.	fem.
nom.	–	–
acc.	ἐμαυτόν	ἐμαυτήν
gen.	ἐμαυτοῦ	ἐμαυτῆς
dat.	ἐμαυτῷ	ἐμαυτῇ

σεαυτόν, σεαυτήν, *yourself*

	masc.	fem.
nom.	–	–
acc.	σεαυτόν	σεαυτήν
gen.	σεαυτοῦ	σεαυτῆς
dat.	σεαυτῷ	σεαυτῇ

ἡμᾶς αὐτούς, ἡμᾶς αὐτάς, *ourselves*

	masc.	fem.
nom.	–	–
acc.	ἡμᾶς αὐτούς	ἡμᾶς αὐτάς
gen.	ἡμῶν αὐτῶν	ἡμῶν αὐτῶν
dat.	ἡμῖν αὐτοῖς	ἡμῖν αὐταῖς

ὑμᾶς αὐτούς, ὑμᾶς αὐτάς, *yourselves*

	masc.	fem.
nom.	–	–
acc.	ὑμᾶς αὐτούς	ὑμᾶς αὐτάς
gen.	ὑμῶν αὐτῶν	ὑμῶν αὐτῶν
dat.	ὑμῖν αὐτοῖς	ὑμῖν αὐταῖς

ἑαυτόν, ἑαυτήν, ἑαυτό, *himself, herself, itself*

	masc.	fem.	neut.
nom.	–	–	–
acc.	ἑαυτόν	ἑαυτήν	ἑαυτό
gen.	ἑαυτοῦ	ἑαυτῆς	ἑαυτοῦ
dat.	ἑαυτῷ	ἑαυτῇ	ἑαυτῷ

ἑαυτούς, ἑαυτάς, ἑαυτά, *themselves*

	masc.	fem.	neut.
nom.	–	–	–
acc.	ἑαυτούς	ἑαυτάς	ἑαυτά
gen.	ἑαυτῶν	ἑαυτῶν	ἑαυτῶν
dat.	ἑαυτοῖς	ἑαυταῖς	ἑαυτοῖς

αὑτόν, αὑτήν, αὑτό, *himself, herself, itself*

	masc.	fem.	neut.
nom.	–	–	–
acc.	αὑτόν	αὑτήν	αὑτό
gen.	αὑτοῦ	αὑτῆς	αὑτοῦ
dat.	αὑτῷ	αὑτῇ	αὑτῷ

αὑτούς, αὑτάς, αὑτά, *themselves*

	masc.	fem.	neut.
nom.	–	–	–
acc.	αὑτούς	αὑτάς	αὑτά
gen.	αὑτῶν	αὑτῶν	αὑτῶν
dat.	αὑτοῖς	αὑταῖς	αὑτοῖς

Note 1 ἑαυτόν, ἑαυτήν, ἑαυτό, and αὑτόν, αὑτήν, αὑτό are alternative forms: there is no difference in meaning.

Note 2 Another reflexive pronoun you have met is ἀλληλούς, *each other*. This declines like καλ-ός ή όν, but is found only in the accusative, genitive and dative plural.

Note 3 Be careful to distinguish between forms of αὐτόν, *him*, etc. and αὑτόν, *himself*, etc.

Verbs

The present tense

Present active

παύω, *I stop*

	indicative	imperative
sing.	παύ-ω	
	παύ-εις	παῦ-ε, *stop!* (s.)
	παύ-ει	παυ-έτω,* *let him/her stop!*
pl.	παύ-ομεν	
	παύ-ετε	παύ-ετε, *stop!* (pl.)
	παύ-ουσι(ν)	παυ-όντων,* *let them stop!*

infinitive†

παύ-ειν, *to stop*

participle

παύ-ων, παύ-ουσα, παῦ-ον (παυοντ-), *stopping*

Note 1 The movable nu (ν) of παύ-ουσι(ν) and various other verb forms is often (but not always) used when the verb in question comes at the end of a sentence or precedes a vowel (διώκουσιν οἱ ἄνδρες, *the men are pursuing*). It does not affect the meaning of the verb, nor is it wrong to omit it.

Note 2 Remember that παύω (etc.) may be translated *I stop*, *I am stopping*, or *I do stop*, according to context.

Note 3 παύων, παύουσα, παῦον (παυοντ-) is laid out in full on p. 66.

ποιέω, *I make, do* (contract verb in ε)

	indicative			imperative		
sing.	ποιέ-ω	→	ποιῶ			
	ποιέ-εις	→	ποιεῖς	ποίε-ε	→	ποίει
	ποιέ-ει	→	ποιεῖ	ποιε-έτω*	→	ποιείτω
pl.	ποιέ-ομεν	→	ποιοῦμεν			
	ποιέ-ετε	→	ποιεῖτε	ποιε-έτε	→	ποιεῖτε
	ποιέ-ουσι(ν)	→	ποιοῦσι(ν)	ποιέ-οντων*	→	ποιούντων

infinitive†

ποιέ-ειν → ποιεῖν

participle

ποιέ-ων ουσα ον (-οντ-) → ποιῶν, ποιοῦσα, ποιοῦν (ποιουντ-)

Note 1 Note the difference in accentuation between ποιεῖ, *(s)he does* and ποίει, *do!* (s.).

Note 2 **For information**: the verb πλέω contracts only when the verb ending begins with ε. Thus:
πλέω, πλεῖς, πλεῖ, πλέομεν, πλεῖτε, πλέουσι(ν)
infinitive: πλεῖν
imperatives: πλεῖ, πλείτω, πλεῖτε, πλεόντων
participle: πλέων, πλέουσα, πλέον (πλεοντ-)

Note 3 ποιῶν, ποιοῦσα, ποιοῦν (ποιουντ-) is laid out in full on p. 67.

τιμάω, *I honour* (contract verb in α)

	indicative			imperative		
sing.	τιμά-ω	→	τιμῶ			
	τιμά-εις	→	τιμᾷς	τίμα-ε	→	τίμα
	τιμά-ει	→	τιμᾷ	τιμα-έτω*	→	τιμάτω
pl.	τιμά-ομεν	→	τιμῶμεν			
	τιμά-ετε	→	τιμᾶτε	τιμά-ετε	→	τιμᾶτε
	τιμά-ουσι(ν)	→	τιμῶσι(ν)	τιμα-όντων*	→	τιμώντων

infinitive†
τιμά-ειν → τιμᾶν

participle
τιμά-ων ουσα ον (-οντ-) → τιμῶν, τιμῶσα, τιμῶν (τιμωντ-)

Note 1 There is no iota subscript in the infinitive.

Note 2 τιμῶν, τιμῶσα, τιμῶν (τιμωντ-) is laid out in full on p. 67.

δηλόω, *I show, reveal* (contract verb in ο)

	indicative imperative					
sing.	δηλό-ω	→	δηλῶ			
	δηλό-εις	→	δηλοῖς	δήλο-ε	→	δήλου
	δηλό-ει	→	δηλοῖ	δηλο-έτω*	→	δηλούτω
pl.	δηλό-ομεν	→	δηλοῦμεν			
	δηλό-ετε	→	δηλοῦτε	δηλό-ετε	→	δηλοῦτε
	δηλό-ουσι(ν)	→	δηλοῦσι(ν)	δηλο-όντων*	→	δηλούντων

infinitive†
δηλό-ειν → δηλοῦν

participle
δηλό-ων -ουσα -ον (-οντ-) → δηλῶν, δηλοῦσα, δηλοῦν (δηλουντ-)

Note 1 There is no iota subscript in the infinitive.

Note 2 The only ο contract active verbs met in *G&E* Sections 1–9 are δηλόω, *I show* and ἐλευθερόω, *I free*.

Note 3 δηλῶν, δηλοῦσα, δηλοῦν (δηλουντ-) is laid out in full on p. 68.

Present middle

παύομαι, *I stop (myself)*

	indicative	imperative
sing.	παύ-ομαι	
	παύ-ῃ (or παύ-ει)	παύ-ου, *stop!* (s.)
	παύ-εται	παυέσθω,* *let him/her stop!*
pl.	παυ-όμεθα	
	παύ-εσθε	παύ-εσθε, *stop!* (pl.)
	παύ-ονται	παυ-έσθων,* *let them stop!*

infinitive†
παύ-εσθαι, *to stop*

participle
παυ-όμεν-ος η ον, *stopping*

φοβέομαι, *I fear* (contract verb in ε)

	indicative			imperative		
sing.	φοβέ-ομαι	→	φοβοῦμαι			
	φοβέ-ῃ	→	φοβῇ	φοβέ-ου	→	φοβοῦ
	φοβέ-εται	→	φοβεῖται	φοβε-έσθω*	→	φοβείσθω
pl.	φοβε-όμεθα	→	φοβούμεθα			
	φοβέ-εσθε	→	φοβεῖσθε	φοβέ-εσθε	→	φοβεῖσθε
	φοβέ-ονται	→	φοβοῦνται	φοβε-έσθων*	→	φοβείσθων

infinitive†
φοβέ-εσθαι → φοβεῖσθαι

participle
φοβέ-ομεν-ος η ον → φοβούμεν-ος η ον

θεάομαι, *I watch* (contract verb in -α-)

	indicative			imperative		
sing.	θεά-ομαι	→	θεῶμαι			
	θεά-ῃ	→	θεᾷ	θεά-ου	→	θεῶ
	θεά-εται	→	θεᾶται	θεα-έσθω*	→	θεάσθω
pl.	θεα-όμεθα	→	θεώμεθα			
	θεά-εσθε	→	θεᾶσθε	θεά-εσθε	→	θεᾶσθε
	θεά-ονται	→	θεῶνται	θεα-έσθων*	→	θεάσθων

infinitive†

θεά-εσθαι → θεᾶσθαι

participle

θεά-ομεν-ος η ον → θεώμεν-ος η ον

Note 1 The only α contract middle verbs met in *G&E* Sections 1–9 are θεάομαι, *I watch*; πειράομαι†, *I try*; and χράομαι†, *I use.*

Note 2 **For information**: χράομαι follows a slightly different pattern of conjugation from most α contract verbs: η is found instead of α when the verb ending begins with ε. Thus:
χρῶμαι, χρῇ, χρῆται, χρώμεθα, χρῆσθε, χρῶνται
imperatives: χρῶ, χρήσθω, χρῆσθε, χρήσθων
infinitive: χρῆσθαι; participle: χρώμεν-ος η ον

δουλόομαι, *I enslave* (contract verb in ο)*

	indicative			imperative		
sing.	δουλό-ομαι	→	δουλοῦμαι			
	δουλό-ῃ	→	δουλοῖ	δουλό-ου	→	δουλοῦ
	δουλό-εται	→	δουλοῦται	δουλο-έσθω*	→	δουλούσθω
pl.	δουλο-όμεθα	→	δουλούμεθα			
	δουλό-εσθε	→	δουλοῦσθε	δουλό-εσθε	→	δουλοῦσθε
	δουλό-ονται	→	δουλοῦνται	δουλο-έσθων*	→	δουλούσθων

infinitive

δουλό-εσθαι → δουλοῦσθαι

participle

δουλό-ομεν-ος η ον → δουλούμεν-ος η ον

Note 1 δουλόυμαι is the only middle ο contract verb met in *G&E* Sections 1–9.

Present active optative[†]

παύω, *I stop*

sing.	παύ-οιμι
	παύ-οις
	παύ-οι
pl.	παύ-οιμεν
	παύ-οιτε
	παύ-οιεν

ποιέω, *I make, do* (contract verb in ε)

sing.	ποιε-οίην	→	ποιοίην
	ποιε-οίης	→	ποιοίης
	ποιε-οίη	→	ποιοίη
pl.	ποιέ-οιμεν	→	ποιοῖμεν
	ποιέ-οιτε	→	ποιοῖτε
	ποιέ-οιεν	→	ποιοῖεν

τιμάω, *I honour* (contract verb in α)

sing.	τιμα-οίην	→	τιμῴην
	τιμα-οίης	→	τιμῴης
	τιμα-οίη	→	τιμῴη
pl.	τιμά-οιμεν	→	τιμῷμεν
	τιμά-οιτε	→	τιμῷτε
	τιμά-οιεν	→	τιμῷεν

δηλόω, *I show, reveal* (contract verb in ο)

sing.	δηλο-οίην	→	δηλοίην
	δηλο-οίης	→	δηλοίης
	δηλο-οίη	→	δηλοίη
pl.	δηλό-οιμεν	→	δηλοῖμεν
	δηλό-οιτε	→	δηλοῖτε
	δηλό-οιεν	→	δηλοῖεν

Note 1 In the singular the endings of contract verbs differ from those of non-contract verbs.

Note 2 For uses of the optative, see *G&E*, p. 169 §186.

Note 3 **For information**: the present optative of πλέω, *I sail*, is: πλέοιμι, πλέοις, πλέοι, πλέοιμεν, πλέοιτε, πλέοιεν.

Note 4 You may be asked to recognise, but not to translate or produce, present optative forms in Part 2 of the examination.

Present middle optative*

παύομαι, *I stop*

sing.	παυ-οίμην
	παύ-οιο
	παύ-οιτο
pl.	παυ-οίμεθα
	παύ-οισθε
	παύ-οιντο

ποιέομαι, *I make, do* (contract verb in ε)

sing.	ποιε-οίμην	→	ποιοίμην
	ποιέ-οιο	→	ποιοῖο
	ποιέ-οιτο	→	ποιοῖτο
pl.	ποιε-οίμεθα	→	ποιοίμεθα
	ποιέ-οισθε	→	ποιοῖσθε
	ποιέ-οιντο	→	ποιοῖντο

θεάομαι, *I watch* (contract verb in α)

sing.	θεα-οίμην	→	θεῴμην
	θεά-οιο	→	θεῷο
	θεά-οιτο	→	θεῷτο
pl.	θεα-οίμεθα	→	θεῴμεθα
	θεά-οισθε	→	θεῷσθε
	θεά-οιντο	→	θεῷντο

δουλόομαι, *I enslave* (contract verb in ο)

sing.	δουλο-οίμην	→	δουλοίμην
	δουλό-οιο	→	δουλοῖο
	δουλό-οιτο	→	δουλοῖτο
pl.	δουλο-οίμεθα	→	δουλοίμεθα
	δουλό-οισθε	→	δουλοῖσθε
	δουλό-οιντο	→	δουλοῖντο

Note 1 As with active optatives, you may be asked to recognise but not to translate or produce a middle optative form in the examination.

Note 2 For uses of the optative, see *G&E*, p. 169 §186.

Note 3 Optatives of irregular and athematic verbs are included on pp. 56–9 and pp. 64–5 below.

The imperfect tense

Imperfect active

παύω, *I stop*

sing.	ἔ-παυ-ον
	ἔ-παυ-ες
	ἔ-παυ-ε(ν)
pl.	ἐ-παύ-ομεν
	ἐ-παύ-ετε
	ἔ-παυ-ον

ποιέω, *I make, do* (contract verb in ε)

sing.	ἐ-ποίε-ον	→	ἐποίουν
	ἐ-ποίε-ες	→	ἐποίεις
	ἐ-ποίε-ε	→	ἐποίει
pl.	ἐ-ποιέ-ομεν	→	ἐποιοῦμεν
	ἐ-ποιέ-ετε	→	ἐποιεῖτε
	ἐ-ποιέ-ον	→	ἐποίουν

τιμάω, *I honour* (contract verb in α)

sing.	ἐ-τίμα-ον	→	ἐτίμων
	ἐ-τίμα-ες	→	ἐτίμας
	ἐ-τίμα-ε	→	ἐτίμα
pl.	ἐ-τιμά-ομεν	→	ἐτιμῶμεν
	ἐ-τιμά-ετε	→	ἐτιμᾶτε
	ἐ-τίμα-ον	→	ἐτίμων

δηλόω, *I show, reveal* (contract verb in ο)

sing.	ἐ-δήλο-ον	→	ἐδήλουν
	ἐ-δήλο-ες	→	ἐδήλους
	ἐ-δήλο-ε	→	ἐδήλου
pl.	ἐ-δηλό-ομεν	→	ἐδηλοῦμεν
	ἐ-δηλό-ετε	→	ἐδηλοῦτε
	ἐ-δήλο-ον	→	ἐδήλουν

Note 1 Take care not to confuse imperfect and second aorist forms since these share the same endings. The imperfect, unlike the second aorist, is based on the *present* stem.

Note 2 Few verbs show any irregularity in the imperfect. These are listed on pp. 56–9.

Note 3 There is no imperfect infinitive or participle.

Note 4 For ways of translating the imperfect, see *G&E*, p. 93 §103 and p. 98 §109.

Note 5 The verbs above begin with consonants and so take a 'syllabic' augment: ἐ-. Remember that verbs beginning with a vowel take a 'temporal' augment; i.e. the initial vowel lengthens if it can. For the rules of augmentation, see Appendix One.

Note 6 **For information**: ὁράω and πλέω have slightly quirky imperfects. As in the present, πλέω contracts only when the ending begins with an ε: see p. 35, note 2 (top of page). Thus in the imperfect: ἔπλεον, ἔπλεις, ἔπλει, ἐπλέομεν, ἐπλεῖτε, ἔπλεον.
ὁράω takes a double augment, both 'syllabic', ἐ-, and 'temporal': ο → ω. Thus: ἑώρα-ον, etc., contracts to ἑώρων, ἑώρας, ἑώρα, ἑωρῶμεν, ἑωρᾶτε, ἑώρων.

Imperfect middle

παύομαι, *I stop*

sing.	ἐ-παυ-όμην
	ἐ-παύ-ου
	ἐ-παύ-ετο
pl.	ἐ-παυ-όμεθα
	ἐ-παύ-εσθε
	ἐ-παύ-οντο

φοβέομαι, *I fear* (contract verb in ε)

sing.	ἐ-φοβε-όμην	→	ἐφοβούμην
	ἐ-φοβέ-ου	→	ἐφοβοῦ
	ἐ-φοβέ-ετο	→	ἐφοβεῖτο
pl.	ἐ-φοβε-όμεθα	→	ἐφοβούμεθα
	ἐ-φοβέ-εσθε	→	ἐφοβεῖσθε
	ἐ-φοβέ-οντο	→	ἐφοβοῦντο

θεάομαι, *I watch* (contract verb in α)

sing.	ἐ-θεα-όμην	→	ἐθεώμην
	ἐ-θεά-ου	→	ἐθεῶ
	ἐ-θεά-ετο	→	ἐθεᾶτο
pl.	ἐ-θεα-όμεθα	→	ἐθεώμεθα
	ἐ-θεά-εσθε	→	ἐθεᾶσθε
	ἐ-θεά-οντο	→	ἐθεῶντο

δουλόομαι*, *I enslave* (contract verb in ο)

sing.	ἐ-δουλο-όμην	→	ἐδουλούμην
	ἐ-δουλό-ου	→	ἐδουλοῦ
	ἐ-δουλό-ετο	→	ἐδουλοῦτο
pl.	ἐ-δουλο-όμεθα	→	ἐδουλούμεθα
	ἐ-δουλό-εσθε	→	ἐδουλοῦσθε
	ἐ-δουλό-οντο	→	ἐδουλοῦντο

Note 1 See notes 1–5 about the imperfect tense on pp. 40–1.

Note 2 **For information:** As in the present, χράομαι, *I use*, behaves slightly differently from other α contract verbs (p. 37, note 2). Its imperfect forms are:
ἐχρώμην, ἐχρῶ, ἐχρῆτο, ἐχρώμεθα, ἐχρῆσθε, ἐχρῶντο.

Note 3 Imperfects of irregular verbs (εἰμί, εἶμι, οἶδα, φημί) and athematic verbs (δύναμαι, ἀνίσταμαι) are listed on pp. 56–9 and 64–5 below.

The aorist

There is no fail-safe method of predicting which verbs have a first (weak) aorist and which a second (strong) aorist. First aorists, which the majority of verbs display, are dealt with on pp. 43–7, second aorists on pp. 48–9 and root aorists on p. 50. The more you read, the more familiar you will become with the aorist forms of all verbs.

Remember that the crosses (†) and asterisks (*) mark forms which you will not be required to reproduce in the respective sections of the examination.

First aorists are formed in the following ways.

First (weak) aorists

Non-contract verbs with vowel stems

In the case of our model verb παύω, *I stop*, we take the present stem παυ-, and add a σ to form the aorist stem, παυσ-. To form a *finite* verb (a form such as 'I stopped', 'he stopped') the stem is augmented, ἐ-παυσ-, and then the appropriate ending is added. (Note that first aorist stems are also used *without* augments to form the aorist imperative, infinitive and participle.)

present			**aorist**
κελεύ-ω, *I order*	κελευ + σ	→	ἐ-κέλευσ-α, *I ordered*
λύ-ω, *I release*	λυ + σ	→	ἔ-λυσ-α, *I released*
ἀκού-ω, *I hear*	ἀκου + σ	→	ἤκουσ-α, *I heard*

Contract verbs

To form the aorist stem of a contract verb, take the present stem, lengthen the last vowel, then add the σ. ε and α lengthen to η, ο lengthens to ω:

present		**aorist stem**	**aorist**
φιλέ-ω, *I love*	(ε → η)	φιλησ-	ἐ-φίλησ-α, *I loved*
τιμά-ω, *I honour*	(α → η)	τιμησ-	ἐ-τίμησ-α, *I honoured*
δηλό-ω, *I show*	(ο → ω)	δηλωσ-	ἐ-δήλωσ-α, *I showed*

Contract verbs whose stems end in εα or ρα

One group of contract verbs is slightly more complex. These are contract verbs in α, where the α is preceded in the stem by an ε or ρ. When these conditions are met, the α remains an α rather than lengthening into an η as might be expected (although the α preceding the σ would have been pronounced as a long vowel: ᾱ e.g. ἔδρᾱσα). Observe the following:

present	**aorist stem**	**aorist**
δράω, *I do, act*	δρασ-	ἔδρασα, *I did, acted*
ἐάω†, *I allow*	ἐασ-*	εἴασα*, *I allowed*
θεάομαι, *I watch*	θεασ-*	ἐθεασάμην*, *I watched*
πειράομαι†, *I try, test*	πειρασ-†	ἐπειρασάμην*, *I tried, tested*

Note 1 χράομαι†, *I use*, is irregular in this respect, its aorist being ἐχρησάμην. See p. 37, note 2 above on the odd behaviour exhibited by χράομαι in the present tense.

Note 2 These verbs follow the same principle in the future: δράσω, ἐάσω, etc.

Verbs with consonant stems

Adding a σ on the end of the present stem to form the aorist stem will often produce a new consonant.

Verbs whose present stems end in β, π or φ (or πτ)

In the case of verbs whose present stems end in β, π or φ (or πτ), these consonants combine with the σ to produce a ψ:

present			**aorist**
πέμπ-ω†, *I send*	πεμπ + σ	→	ἔ-πεμψ-α†, *I sent*
βλέπ-ω, *I look*	βλεπ + σ	→	ἔ-βλεψ-α, *I looked*
γράφ-ομαι*, *I charge*	γραφ + σ	→	ἐ-γραψ-άμην*, *I charged*

(These are *labial* consonants, pronounced on the lips.)

Verbs whose present stems end in γ, κ or χ

In the case of verbs whose present stems end in γ, κ or χ, these consonants combine with the σ to produce a ξ. Verbs whose stems end in -ττ- usually behave in this way too:

present			**aorist**
δέχ-ομαι, *I receive*	δεχ + σ	→	ἐ-δεξ-άμην, *I received*
διώκ-ω†, *I pursue*	διωκ+ σ	→	ἐ-δίωξ-α†, *I pursued*
φυλάττ-ω†, *I guard*	φυλακ + σ	→	ἐ-φύλαξ-α†, *I guarded*

(These are *guttural* or *velar* consonants, pronounced in the throat.)

Verbs whose present stems end in δ, ζ, θ or τ

In the case of verbs whose present stems end in δ, ζ, τ or θ, these consonants drop out altogether and are replaced by the σ:

present			aorist
φροντίζ-ω, *I worry*	φροντιζ + σ	→	ἐ-φρόντισ-α, *I worried*
πείθ-ω, *I persuade*	πειθ + σ	→	ἔ-πεισ-α, *I persuaded*
ᾄδ-ω†, *I sing*	ᾄδ + σ	→	ᾖσα†, *I sang*

(These are *dental* consonants, pronounced on the teeth.)

Verbs whose stems end in λ, μ, ν or ρ

A more awkward group of verbs consists of those whose stems end in ν and μ (*nasal* consonants, pronounced through the nose) or λ and ρ (*liquid* consonants, properly pronounced by running the tongue over the roof of the mouth above the teeth). When a verb's stem ends in ν, μ, λ or ρ, it cannot form its aorist by simply adding a σ. Instead the verb's stem either remains unchanged or, if the final vowel in the present stem is short, it lengthens. Only a few such verbs are met in Sections 1–9 of *G&E*.

present	aorist stem	aorist
ἀποκρίνομαι†, *I answer*	ἀποκριν-†	ἀπεκρινάμην†, *I answered*
ἀποκτείνω, *I kill*	ἀποκτειν-	ἀπέκτεινα
or as a second aorist	ἀποκταν-*	ἀπέκτανον*, *I killed*
διαφθείρω, *I destroy*	διαφθειρ-†	διέφθειρα†, *I destroyed*
μένω, *I stay, wait*	μειν-	ἔμεινα, *I stayed, waited*
οἰκτ(ε)ίρω†, *I pity, lament*	οἰκτ(ε)ιρ-†	ᾤκτ(ε)ιρα†, *I pitied*

Note also how the following two verbs form their aorists.

present	aorist stem	aorist
ἐθέλω, *I wish*	ἐθελησ-*	ἠθέλησα*, *I wished*
μέλλω†, *I intend*	μελλησ-*	ἐμέλλησα*, *I intended*

Unpredictable first aorists

Some verbs met in *G&E* Sections 1–9 have a first aorist but undergo an unpredictable stem change. These are listed below.

present	**aorist stem**	**aorist**
(ἐπ)αἰνέω†, *I praise*	(ἐπ)αἰνεσ-†	(ἐπ)ῄνεσα†, *I praised*
(ἀφ)ἕλκω*, *I drag (off)*	(ἀφ)ἑλκυσ-*	(ἀφ)είλκυσα*, *I dragged (off)*
γελάω†, *I laugh*	γελασ-*	ἐγέλασα*, *I laughed*
καλέω, *I call*	καλεσ-*	ἐκάλεσα*, *I called*
μάχομαι, *I fight*	μαχεσ-	ἐμαχεσάμην, *I fought*
πλέω, *I sail*	πλευσ-	ἔπλευσα, *I sailed*
φθάνω, *I anticipate*	φθασ-*	ἔφθασα*, *I anticipated*

Note 1 σῴζω, *I save*, drops its iota subscript in the aorist to give ἔσωσα, stem σωσ-. ῥίπτω, *I throw*, has the aorist stem ῥιψ- and forms its aorist as ἔρριψα; this duplication of the ρ is regular after the augment for verbs beginning with this letter.

Note 2 Some verbs such as λέγω and ἐρωτάω have both first and second aorists. Such verbs, along with all verbs met in A275 with irregular and quirky aorists, are included in the list of irregular verbs on pp. 60–3 below.

First aorist active

	indicative	**imperative**†
sing.	ἔ-παυσ-α	
	ἔ-παυσ-ας	παῦσ-ον, *stop!* (s.)
	ἔ-παυσ-ε(ν)	παυσ-άτω*, *let him/her stop!*
pl.	ἐ-παύσ-αμεν	
	ἐ-παύσ-ατε	παύσ-ατε, *stop!* (pl.)
	ἔ-παυσ-αν	παυσ-άντων*, *let them stop!*

infinitive†

παῦσ-αι, *to stop*

participle†

παύσ-ας ασα αν (παυσαντ-), *having stopped, on stopping, stopping*

First aorist middle

	indicative	**imperative**†
sing.	ἐ-παυσ-άμην	
	ἐ-παύσ-ω	παῦσ-αι, *stop!* (s.)
	ἐ-παύσ-ατο	παυσ-άσθω*, *let him/her stop!*
pl.	ἐ-παυσ-άμεθα	
	ἐ-παύσ-ασθε	παύσ-ασθε, *stop!* (pl.)
	ἐ-παύσ-αντο	παυσ-άσθων*, *let them stop!*

infinitive†

παύσ-ασθαι, *to stop*

participle†

παυσάμεν-ος η ον, *having stopped, on stopping, stopping*

Note 1 There is no augment on aorist imperatives, infinitives or participles, only on 'finite' forms of the verb: that is, ἔπαυσα, *I stopped*, ἔπαυσας, *you stopped*, etc.

Note 2 The difference between present and aorist imperatives is one of aspect: see *G&E*, pp. 190–1 §200. In practice, it is usually easiest to translate aorist imperatives in the same way as present imperatives. Note that you do not learn how to issue a negative command with aorist aspect. For all negative commands, use μή + present imperative: μὴ παῦε, μὴ παύετε, etc.

Note 3 Note that the form παῦσαι can signify both *to stop* (active infinitive) and *stop!* (middle sing. imperative).

Note 4 First aorist participles are laid out in full on p. 70 below.

Second aorists

The following is a list of second aorist forms met in *G&E* Sections 1–9. As with the first aorist, the augmented stem is used to form the 'finite' forms of the verb: *I led*, *you took*, etc. (Note, however, that it is the unaugmented stem that is used to form the aorist imperative, infinitive and participle.)

present	**aorist stem**	**aorist**
(ἀπ)ἄγω, *I lead, take (away)*	(ἀπ)ἀγαγ-	(ἀπ)ἤγαγον
αἱρέω†, *I take*	ἑλ-	εἷλον
ἀποθνῄσκω, *I die*	ἀποθαν-	ἀπέθανον
ἀφικνέομαι, *I arrive*	ἀφικ-	ἀφικόμην
(ἐκ)βάλλω, *I throw (out)*	βαλ-	(ἐξ)έβαλον
γίγνομαι, *I become*	γεν-	ἐγενόμην
δάκνω†, *I bite, worry*	δακ†-	ἔδακον†
ἕπομαι†, *I follow*	σπ-†	ἑσπόμην†
ἔρχομαι, *I come, go*	ἐλθ-	ἦλθον
ἐρωτάω, *I ask* (also a first aorist	ἐρ- ἐρωτησ-	ἠρόμην ἠρώτησα)
ἐσθίω†, *I eat*	φαγ-†	ἔφαγον†
(ἐξ)εὑρίσκω, *I find (out)*	(ἐξ)εὑρ-	(ἐξ)ηὗρον
ἔχω, *I have*	σχ-	ἔσχον
λαμβάνω, *I take*	λαβ-	ἔλαβον
λανθάνω, *I escape the notice of*	λαθ-	ἔλαθον
λέγω, *I say, speak* (also a first aorist	εἰπ- λεξ-	εἶπον ἔλεξα)
μανθάνω, *I learn*	μαθ-	ἔμαθον
ὁράω, *I see*	ἰδ-	εἶδον
πάσχω, *I suffer*	παθ-	ἔπαθον
πείθομαι, *I believe, trust, obey*	πιθ-	ἐπιθόμην
πίπτω, *I fall*	πεσ-	ἔπεσον
τρέπομαι, *I turn, turn in flight* (also a first aorist	τραπ- τρεψ-	ἐτραπόμην ἐτρεψάμην)
τρέχω, *I run*	δραμ-	ἔδραμον
τυγχάνω, *I happen*	τυχ-	ἔτυχον
φέρω, *I carry* (also a first aorist	ἐνεγκ-	ἤνεγκον ἤνεγκα)
(ἀπο)φεύγω, *I flee* (*escape*)	(ἀπο)φυγ-	(ἀπ)έφυγον

Note 1 ἔρχομαι, *I come/go*, a middle verb in the present, becomes active in the aorist: ἦλθον, *I came/went*, with no change of nuance.

Note 2 The aorist imperatives of ὁράω are most often the middle forms ἰδού and ἰδέσθε.

Note 3 Some aorist stems are borrowed from what were once separate verbs: e.g. λέγω (εἰπ-).

Second aorist active

λαμβάνω, *I take*

	indicative	imperative†
sing.	ἔ-λαβ-ον	
	ἔ-λαβ-ες	λαβ-έ, *take!* (s.)
	ἔ-λαβ-ε(ν)	λαβ-έτω*, *let him/her take!*
pl.	ἐ-λάβ-ομεν	
	ἐ-λάβ-ετε	λάβ-ετε, *take!* (pl.)
	ἔ-λαβ-ον	λαβ-όντων*, *let them take!*

infinitive†
λαβ-εῖν, *to take*

participle†
λαβ-ών οῦσα όν (λαβοντ-), *having taken, on taking, taking*

Second aorist middle

γίγνομαι, *I become*

	indicative	imperative†
sing.	ἐ-γεν-όμην	
	ἐ-γέν-ου	γεν-οῦ, *become!* (s.)
	ἐ-γέν-ετο	γεν-έσθω*, *let him/her become!*
pl.	ἐ-γεν-όμεθα	
	ἐ-γέν-εσθε	γέν-εσθε, *become!* (pl.)
	ἐ-γέν-οντο	γεν-έσθων*, *let them become!*

infinitive†
γεν-έσθαι, *to become*

participle†
γενόμεν-ος η ον, *having become, on becoming, becoming*

Note 1 See notes 1 and 2 on p. 47 above.

Note 2 Second aorist participles decline in the same way as present participles. λαβ-ών οῦσα όν (λαβοντ-) and γενόμεν-ος η ον are set out in full on p. 71 below.

Root aorists†

A very small number of verbs take what is called a 'root' aorist. The only such verbs met in Sections 1–9 of *G&E* are βαίνω, *I go*, and γιγνώσκω, *I know, realise*. Their roots, βα/βη and γνω/γνο, are used to form the aorist indicative, infinitive and participle in the following way.

βαίνω, *I go*

	indicative
sing.	ἔ-βη-ν, *I went*, etc.
	ἔ-βη-ς
	ἔ-βη
pl.	ἔ-βη-μεν
	ἔ-βη-τε
	ἔ-βη-σαν
	infinitive
	βῆ-ναι, *to go*
	participle
	βάς, βᾶσα, βάν (βαντ-), *having gone, on going, going*

γιγνώσκω, *I know, realise*

	indicative
sing.	ἔ-γνω-ν, *I knew, realised*, etc.
	ἔ-γνω-ς
	ἔ-γνω
pl.	ἔ-γνω-μεν
	ἔ-γνω-τε
	ἔ-γνω-σαν
	infinitive
	γνῶ-ναι, *to realise*
	participle
	γνούς, γνοῦσα, γνόν (γνοντ-), *having realised, on realising, realising*

Note 1 The root aorist participle declines in the same way as the first aorist active participle. It is laid out in full on p. 72 below.

Note 2 **For information**: the aorist imperative forms of βαίνω, which do not need to be learnt, are βῆθι, βήτω, βῆτε, βάντων, and those of γιγνώσκω are γνῶθι, γνώτω, γνῶτε, γνόντων.

Note 3 **For information**: other verbs which take root aorists include ἁλίσκομαι, *I am convicted/caught* (ἑάλων, etc.; ἁλῶναι; ἁλούς, ἁλοῦσα, ἁλόν [ἁλοντ-]).

The future tense

The stem of the future is formed in a similar way to the stem of the first aorist (see pp. 43–6 above); that is, a σ is added to the present stem. Thus the future stem of *παύω*, *I stop*, is παυ-σ-; the future stem of κελεύω, *I order*, is κελευ-σ-. To this stem are added the same endings as we find in the present: thus παύσω, *I shall stop*; κελεύσεις, *you will order*; and so on.

Non-contract verbs with vowel stems

As outlined above, verbs like παύω simply add σ to their present stem.

present			future
παύ-ω, *I stop*	παυ + σ	→	παύσ-ω, *I shall stop*

Contract verbs

With contract verbs, the last vowel of the stem is lengthened before the σ is added:
ε and α lengthen to η; ο lengthens to ω:

present		future	
φιλέ-ω, *I love*	(ε → η)	φιλησ-	φιλήσ-ω, *I shall love*
τιμά-ω, *I honour*	(α → η)	τιμησ-	τιμήσ-ω, *I shall honour*
δηλό-ω, *I show*	(ο → ω)	δηλωσ-	δηλώσ-ω, *I shall show*

Contract verbs whose stems end in εα or ρα*

As with the first aorist, when a verb's stem ends in εα or ρα, the alpha does not lengthen into an η (see p. 44 above). As with the aorist, the α preceding the σ would have been pronounced as a long vowel: ᾱ, e.g. δράσω.

present	future
δράω, *I do, act*	δρᾱ́σω, *I shall do, act*
θεάομαι, *I watch*	θεάσομαι, *I shall watch*

You will not be expected to reproduce such futures in the examination.

Verbs with consonant stems

As with the first aorist, the addition of a σ may result in the production of a new consonant.

Verbs whose present stems end in β, π or φ (or πτ)

β, π or φ (and πτ: *labial* consonants) combine with the σ to produce a ψ:

present			**future**
πέμπ-ω†, *I send*	πεμπ + σ†	→	πέμψ-ω†, *I shall send*

Verbs whose present stems end in γ, κ or χ

γ, κ or χ (and usually -ττ-: *guttural* or *velar* consonants) combine with the σ to produce a ξ:

present			**future**
δέχ-ομαι, *I receive*	δεχ + σ	→	δέξ-ομαι, *I shall receive*

Verbs whose present stem ends in δ, ζ, θ or τ

δ, ζ, τ or θ, (*dental* consonants) drop out altogether and are replaced by the σ:

present			**future**
πείθ-ω, *I persuade*	πειθ + σ	→	πείσ-ω, *I shall persuade*

Verbs whose stems end in λ, μ, ν or ϱ*

Verbs whose stems end in ν or μ (*nasal* consonants) or λ or ϱ (*liquid* consonants) cannot form their future stems by simply adding a σ. These commonly become contract verbs in ε with the stem either undergoing a subtle vowel change or remaining the same as the present.

present			**future**
διαφθείϱω, *I destroy*	διαφθεϱέω	→	διαφθεϱῶ, *I shall destroy*
μένω, *I wait*	μενέω	→	μενῶ, *I shall wait*

You will not be expected to reproduce such futures in the examination.

Verbs whose stems end in ίζω*

Verbs which end in ίζω generally become contract verbs in ε in the future (and are thus conjugated like ποιέω), the ζ dropping out:

present			**future**
ἐλπίζω†, *I hope*	ἐλπιέω	→	ἐλπιῶ*, *I shall hope*
νομίζω†, *I think*	νομιέω	→	νομιῶ†, *I shall think*
φϱοντίζω, *I worry*	φϱοντιέω	→	φϱοντιῶ*, *I shall worry*

You will not be expected to reproduce such futures in the examination.

Verbs which display middle endings in the future

Note, too, that some active verbs (both regular and irregular) display middle endings in the future, but with no change of nuance.

present	future
ἀκούω, *I hear*	ἀκούσομαι, *I shall hear*
μανθάνω, *I learn*	μαθήσομαι, *I shall learn*
πάσχω, *I suffer*	πείσομαι, *I shall suffer*

Verbs with irregular futures

Finally, some verbs simply have irregular futures which have to be learnt. Below is a full list of the irregular and unexpected futures to which you are introduced in Sections 1–9 of *G&E*.

present	**future**
ἀκούω, *I hear*	ἀκούσομαι
βαίνω, *I go*	βήσομαι
βοάω, *I shout*	βοήσομαι
γιγνώσκω, *I learn*	γνώσομαι
διαφθείρω, *I destroy*	διαφθερέω → διαφθερῶ
ἔρχομαι, *I come, go*	εἶμι or ἐλεύσομαι*
λαμβάνω, *I take*	λήψομαι
λανθάνω, *I escape the notice of*	λήσω†
λέγω, *I say, speak*	ἐρέω → ἐρῶ† or λέξω
μανθάνω, *I learn*	μαθήσομαι
μένω, *I wait*	μενέω → μενῶ
νομίζω, *I think*	νομιέω → νομιῶ
ὁράω, *I see*	ὄψομαι
πάσχω, *I suffer*	πείσομαι†
σιωπάω, *I am silent*	σιωπησομαι
φέρω, *I carry*	οἴσω†
φεύγω, *I flee*	φεύξομαι

Future active

παύω, *I stop*

sing.	παύσ-ω
	παύσ-εις
	παύσ-ει
pl.	παύσ-ομεν
	παύσ-ετε
	παύσ-ουσι(ν)
	infinitive†
	παύσ-ειν

Future middle

παύομαι, *I stop (myself)*

sing.	παύσ-ομαι
	παύσ-ῃ (or παύσ-ει)
	παύσ-εται
pl.	παυσ-όμεθα
	παύσ-εσθε
	παύσ-ονται
	infinitive†
	παύσ-εσθαι

Note 1 Use of the future infinitive: for the purposes of this module, you need note the use of the future infinitive after the following verbs only: ἐλπίζω†, *I hope/expect to*; μέλλω†, *I am about to*; ὑπισχνέομαι†, *I promise to*. See *G&E*, p. 200 §208(c).

Irregular verbs

εἰμί, *I am*

present

	indicative	**imperative**†	**optative***
sing.	εἰμί		εἴην
	εἶ	ἴσθι, *be!* (s.)	εἴης
	ἐστί(ν)	ἔστω*, *let him/her be!*	εἴη
pl.	ἐσμέν		εἶμεν
	ἐστέ	ἔστε, *be!* (pl.)	εἶτε
	εἰσί(ν)	ἔστων*, *let them be!*	εἶεν

infinitive†

εἶναι, *to be*

participle

ὤν, οὖσα, ὄν (ὀντ-), *being*

	imperfect
sing.	ἦ(ν)
	ἦσθα
	ἦν
pl.	ἦμεν
	ἦτε
	ἦσαν

	future
sing.	ἔσομαι
	ἔσῃ (or ἔσει)
	ἔσται
pl.	ἐσόμεθα
	ἔσεσθε
	ἔσονται

infinitive†

ἔσεσθαι

Note 1 ὤν, οὖσα, ὄν (ὀντ-) is set out in full on p. 66 below.

Note 2 Both ὄντων and ἔστων are found as the third person plural imperative.

εἶμι, *I shall go*

	present		
	indicative	**imperative**†	**optative***
sing.	εἶμι		ἴοιμι
	εἶ	ἴθι, *go!* (s.)	ἴοις
	εἶσι(ν)	ἴτω*, *let him/her go!*	ἴοι
pl.	ἴμεν		ἴοιμεν
	ἴτε	ἴτε, *go!* (pl.)	ἴοιτε
	ἴασι(ν)	ἰόντων*, *let them go!*	ἴοιεν

infinitive†
ἰέναι, *to go*

participle
ἰών, ἰοῦσα, ἰόν (ἰοντ-), *going*

	imperfect†
sing.	ᾖα (or ᾔειν)
	ᾔεισθα (or ᾔεις)
	ᾔει(ν)
pl.	ᾖμεν
	ᾖτε
	ᾖσαν

Note 1 The infinitive, imperative and participle of εἶμι are present in meaning. ἰών, ἰοῦσα, ἰόν (ἰοντ-) declines like all present participles.

Note 2 Be careful not to confuse εἶμι, εἶ, εἶσι with εἰμί, *I am*, εἶ, *you are* and εἰσί, *they are* (with εἶ, only context can help). Also note the differences between ἦσαν, *they were*, and ᾖσαν, which can mean either *they went* (from εἶμι) or *they knew* (from οἶδα).

οἶδα, *I know*

present

	indicative	**imperative**†	**optative***
sing.	οἶδα		εἰδείην
	οἶσθα	ἴσθι, *know!* (s.)	εἰδείης
	οἶδε	ἴστω*, *let him/her/it know!*	εἰδείη
pl.	ἴσμεν		εἰδεῖμεν
	ἴστε	ἴστε, *know!* (pl.)	εἰδεῖτε
	ἴσασι(ν)	ἴστων*, *let them know!*	εἰδεῖεν

infinitive†

εἰδέναι, *to know*

participle†

εἰδώς, εἰδυῖα, εἰδός (εἰδοτ-), *knowing*

imperfect†

sing.	ᾔδη (or ᾔδειν*)
	ᾔδησθα (or ᾔδεις*)
	ᾔδει(ν)
pl.	ᾖσμεν
	ᾖστε
	ᾖσαν (or ᾔδεσαν)

future*

sing.	εἴσομαι	or	εἰδήσω
	εἴσῃ (or εἴσει)	or	εἰδήσεις
	εἴσεται	or	εἰδήσει
pl.	εἰσόμεθα	or	εἰδήσομεν
	εἴσεσθε	or	εἰδήσετε
	εἴσονται	or	εἰδήσουσι(ν)

future infinitive*

εἴσεσθαι or εἰδήσειν

Note 1 **For information**: it is because οἶδα is in fact a perfect form that its participle looks unusual. (Do not let this affect the way you translate it, however.) Like all active participles, εἰδώς, εἰδυῖα, εἰδός (εἰδοτ-) is declined in the same way as πᾶς, πᾶσα, πᾶν (παντ-).

Note 2 **For information**: the masculine and neuter dative plural of εἰδώς is εἰδόσι(ν).

φημί, *I say*†

	present		
	indicative	**imperative**	**optative***
sing.	φημί		φαίην
	φής or φῄς	φαθί, *say!* (s.)	φαίης
	φησί(ν)	φάτω*, *let him/her/it say!*	φαίη
pl.	φαμέν		φαίμεν
	φατέ	φάτε, *say!* (pl.)	φαίτε
	φασί(ν)	φάντων*, *let them say!*	φαίεν

infinitive

φάναι, *to say*

participle

φάσκ-ων ουσα ον (φασκοντ-) or φάς, φᾶσα, φάν (φαντ-), *saying*

	imperfect
sing.	ἔφην
	ἔφησθα (or ἔφης)
	ἔφη
pl.	ἔφαμεν
	ἔφατε
	ἔφασαν

	future (regular)
sing.	φήσω
	φήσεις
	φήσει
pl.	φήσομεν
	φήσετε
	φήσουσι(ν)

	aorist (regular)*
sing.	ἔφησα
	ἔφησας
	ἔφησε(ν)
pl.	ἐφήσαμεν
	ἐφήσατε
	ἔφησαν

List of irregular verbs

This is a list of all the verbs from Sections 1–9 of *G&E* which have an irregular or unexpected future and/or aorist. Please note that your books have not informed you of a number of the future and aorist forms given below, and so many are given **for information** only. (You will find separate lists of the irregular aorist and future forms you have actually met in *Reading Greek* in the sections on the formation of the aorist and future above.) Bear in mind, too, that the emphasis of the module is on recognising rather than reproducing forms – a glance at the Specimen Examination Paper should allow you to decide how much emphasis is put on irregular forms, and so how much time you should spend on learning them.

Remember that in addition to the verbs listed here you will also be expected to be familiar with the formation of the future and aorist of contract verbs, compound verbs, and so on.

present	**future**	**aorist stem**	**aorist**
ἄγω, *I lead, take*	ἄξω	ἀγαγ-	ἤγαγον
ᾄδω (ἀείδω)†, *I sing*	ᾄσομαι*	ᾀσ-†	ᾖσα†
(ἐπ)αἰνέω,† *I praise*	(ἐπ)αἰνέσω*	(ἐπ)αἰνεσ-†	(ἐπ)ῄνεσα†
αἱρέω, *I take*	αἱρήσω	ἑλ-	εἷλον
ἀκούω, *I hear, listen (to)*	ἀκούσομαι	ἀκουσ-	ἤκουσα
ἀνίσταμαι[1]†, *I get up, emigrate*	ἀναστήσομαι*	ἀναστησ-*	ἀνέστην[2]*
ἀποθνῄσκω, *I die*	ἀποθανέομαι*	ἀποθαν-	ἀπέθανον
ἀποκρίνομαι†, *I answer*	ἀποκρινέομαι*	ἀποκριν-†	ἀπεκρινάμην†
ἀποκτείνω, *I kill*	ἀποκτενέω*	ἀποκτειν- ἀποκταν-*	ἀπέκτεινα ἀπέκτανον*
ἀφικνέομαι, *I arrive*	ἀφίξομαι*	ἀφικ-	ἀφικόμην
βαίνω, *I go*	βήσομαι	βα-†	ἔβην[3]†
(ἐκ)βάλλω, *I throw (out)*	(ἐκ)βαλέω*	(ἐκ)βαλ-	(ἐξ)έβαλον
βούλομαι†, *I wish*	βουλήσομαι*	–	ἐβουλήθην[2]*
γελάω†, *I laugh*	γελάσομαι*	γελασ-*	ἐγέλασα*
γίγνομαι, *I become*	γενήσομαι*	γεν-	ἐγενόμην
γιγνώσκω, *I learn*	γνώσομαι	γνο-	ἔγνων[3]†

present	future	aorist stem	aorist
δάκνω†, *I bite*	δήξομαι*	δακ-†	ἔδακον†
δεῖ†, *it is necessary*	δεήσει*	δεησ-*	ἐδέησε*
διαφθείρω, *I destroy*	διαφθερέω	διαφθειρ-†	διέφθειρα†
δοκέω†, *I seem*	δόξω*	δοξ-*	ἔδοξα*
δράω, *I do, act*	δράσω	δρασ-	ἔδρασα
δύναμαι[1]†, *I am able*	δυνήσομαι*	–	ἐδυνήθην[2]*
ἐάω†, *I allow*	ἐάσω*	ἐασ-*	εἴασα*
ἐθέλω†, *I wish*	ἐθελήσω*	ἐθελησ-*	ἠθέλησα*
(ἀφ)ἕλκω*, *I drag (off)*	(ἀφ)ἕλξω* ((ἀφ)ἑλκύσω)*	(ἀφ)ἑλκυσ-*	(ἀφ)εἵλκυσα*
ἐλπίζω†, *I hope*	ἐλπιέω*	ἐλπισ-†	ἤλπισα†
ἐπίσταμαι[1]†, *I know*	ἐπιστήσομαι*	–	ἠπιστήθην[2]*
ἕπομαι†, *I follow*	ἕψομαι*	σπ-†	ἑσπόμην†
ἔρχομαι, *I come, go*	ἐλεύσομαι* (εἶμι)	ἐλθ-	ἦλθον
ἐρωτάω, *I ask*	ἐρήσομαι* ἐρωτήσω	ἐρ- ἐρωτησ-	ἠρόμην ἠρώτησα
ἐσθίω†, *I eat*	ἔδομαι†	φαγ-†	ἔφαγον†
(ἐξ)ευρίσκω, *I find (out)*	(ἐξ)ευρήσω*	(ἐξ)εὑρ-	(ἐξ)ηὗρον
ἔχω, *I have*	ἕξω*	σχ-	ἔσχον
ἥδομαι†, *I enjoy*	ἡσθήσομαι*	–	ἥσθην[2]*
θεάομαι, *I watch*	θεάσομαι*	θεασ-*	ἐθεασάμην*
καθίζω, *I sit down*	καθιέω* (καθίσω)	καθισ-	ἐκάθισα
καλέω, *I call*	καλέω*	καλεσ-*	ἐκάλεσα*
λαμβάνω, *I take*	λήψομαι	λαβ-	ἔλαβον
λανθάνω, *I escape the notice of*	λήσω†	λαθ-	ἔλαθον
λέγω, *I say, speak*	ἐρέω† λέξω	εἰπ- λεξ-	εἶπον ἔλεξα

present	future	aorist stem	aorist
μανθάνω, *I learn*	μαθήσομαι	μαθ-	ἔμαθον
μάχομαι, *I fight*	μαχέ(σ)ομαι*	μαχεσ-	ἐμαχεσάμην
μέλλω†, *I intend*	μελλήσω*	μελλησ-*	ἐμέλλησα*
μένω, *I stay, I wait*	μενέω	μειν-	ἔμεινα
νομίζω, *I think*	νομιέω	νομισ-	ἐνόμισα
οἰκτ(ε)ίρω†, *I pity, lament*	οἰκτιρέω*	οἰκτ(ε)ιρ-†	ᾤκτ(ε)ιρα†
οἴομαι†, *I think* (usually contracts as οἶμαι)	οἰήσομαι*	–	ᾠήθην[2]*
ὁράω, *I see*	ὄψομαι	ἰδ-[4]	εἶδον
ὀφείλω*, *I owe*	ὀφειλήσω*	ὀφελ-*	ὤφελον* (ὠφείλησα)
πάσχω, *I suffer*	πείσομαι†	παθ-	ἔπαθον
πείθομαι, *I believe, trust, obey*	πείσομαι	πιθ-	ἐπιθόμην
πείθω, *I persuade*	πείσω	πεισ- (πιθ-)*	ἔπεισα (ἔπιθον)*
πειράομαι†, *I try, test*	πειράσομαι†	πειρασ-†	ἐπειρασάμην†
πίπτω, *I fall*	πεσέομαι*	πεσ-	ἔπεσον
πλέω, *I sail*	πλεύσομαι*	πλευσ-	ἔπλευσα
πορεύομαι, *I march, journey*	πορεύ(θη)σομαι*	(πορευσ-)	ἐπορεύθην[2]*
σκοπέω, *I view*	σκέψομαι*	σκεψ-*	ἐσκεψάμην*
σπένδω*, *I pour a libation*	σπείσω*	σπεισ-*	ἔσπεισα*
σῴζω, *I save*	σώσω*	σωσ-*	ἔσωσα*
τρέπομαι, *I turn (in flight)*	τρέψομαι	τραπ-	ἐτραπόμην
τρέχω, *I run*	δραμέομαι*	δραμ-	ἔδραμον
τυγχάνω, *I happen*	τεύξομαι*	τυχ-	ἔτυχον
τύπτω, *I strike*	τυπτήσω*	τυπτησ-*	ἐτύπτησα*
ὑπισχνέομαι, *I promise*	ὑποσχήσομαι*	ὑποσχ-*	ὑπεσχόμην*

present	future	aorist stem	aorist
φαίνομαι, *I appear, seem*	φανέομαι*	φαν-*	ἐφάνην*
φέρω, *I carry*	οἴσω†	ἐνεγκ-	ἤνεγκον (ἤνεγκα)
φεύγω, *I flee*	φεύξομαι	φυγ-	ἔφυγον
φθάνω, *I anticipate*	φθήσομαι*	φθασ-*	ἔφθασα* ἔφθην[2]*
φροντίζω, *I worry*	φροντιέω*	φροντισ-	ἐφρόντισα
χράομαι†, *I use*	χρήσομαι*	χρησ-*	ἐχρησάμην*
χρή†, *it is necessary*	χρήσει*	–	(ἐ)χρῆν* (impf.)

[1] So-called 'athematic' verbs: see pp. 64–5.

[2] Deponent: these aorist forms are not met until Section 17D of *G&E* and need not be learnt.

[3] Root aorist: see p. 50.

[4] Aorist imperative in Attic Greek is ἰδοὐ, ἰδέσθε (as if middle): ἰδέ, ἰδέτε is found in some Greek authors, such as Homer.

Note 1 The endings of the verbs in the aorist form indicate whether a given verb is first active (-α), first middle (-αμην), second active (-ον), second middle (-ομην), etc. The aorist stem – without augmentation – is used for aorist infinitives, participles and imperatives.

Note 2 All verbs in the present and future are given in their non-contracted form (where appropriate): e.g. καλέω, *I call/I shall call*, would appear in a text as καλῶ.

Note 3 The four irregular verbs εἰμί, εἶμι, οἶδα and φημί have not been included in this list. These verbs are laid out in full on pp. 56–9 above. The imperfect of these four verbs are the only four irregular imperfects you will be expected to know.

Note 4 **For information**: στένω†, *I groan*, is not included in this list: it has no aorist or future form and appears only in the present and imperfect. Nor is ὀλοφύρομαι*, *I lament*, which appears only rarely outside the present; future: ὀλοφυρέομαι, aorist: ὠλοφυράμην.

Athematic verbs†

'Athematic' is the term used to denote a verb which does not conjugate in the same pattern as παύω/παύομαι. In *G&E* Sections 1–9 you meet a handful of such verbs: δύναμαι, *I am able*; ἀνίσταμαι, *I get up, stand up, emigrate*; and ἐπίσταμαι, *I know how to, understand.*

δύναμαι, *I am able*

	present	
	indicative	**optative***
sing.	δύναμαι	δυναίμην
	δύνασαι	δύναιο
	δύναται	δύναιτο
pl.	δυνάμεθα	δυναίμεθα
	δύνασθε	δύναισθε
	δύνανται	δύναιντο
	infinitive	
	δύνασθαι	
	participle	
	δυνάμεν-ος η ον	

	imperfect
sing.	ἐδυνάμην
	ἐδύνασο (or ἐδύνω*)
	ἐδύνατο
pl.	ἐδυνάμεθα
	ἐδύνασθε
	ἐδύναντο

	future (regular)*
sing.	δυνήσομαι
	δυνήσῃ (or δυνήσει)
	δυνήσεται
pl.	δυνησόμεθα
	δυνήσεσθε
	δυνήσονται

ἀνίσταμαι, *I get up*

	present	
	indicative	**optative***
sing.	ἀνίσταμαι	ἀνισταίμην
	ἀνίστασαι	ἀνίσταιο
	ἀνίσταται	ἀνίσταιτο
pl.	ἀνιστάμεθα	ἀνισταίμεθα
	ἀνίστασθε	ἀνίσταισθε
	ἀνίστανται	ἀνίσταιντο
	infinitive	
	ἀνίστασθαι	
	participle	
	ἀνιστάμεν-ος η ον	

	imperfect*
sing.	ἀνιστάμην
	ἀνίστασο
	ἀνίστατο
pl.	ἀνιστάμεθα
	ἀνίστασθε
	ἀνίσταντο

	future (regular)*
sing.	ἀνιστήσομαι
	ἀνιστήσῃ (or ἀνιστήσει)
	ἀνιστήσεται
pl.	ἀνιστησόμεθα
	ἀνιστήσεσθε
	ἀνιστήσονται

Note 1 ἐπίσταμαι, *I know how to, understand*, is conjugated like ἀνίσταμαι. These three verbs are in fact middle verbs and their participles decline like all middle participles.

Note 2 **For information**: you also meet parts of the 'athematic' verb τίθημι, *I put, place*; for the declension of this verb, see *G&E*, pp. 251–3.

Participles

Present active participles

ὤν, οὖσα, ὄν (ὀντ-), *being* (from εἰμί)

sing.

	masc.	**fem.**	**neut.**
nom.	ὤν	οὖσ-α	ὄν
acc.	ὄντ-α	οὖσ-αν	ὄν
gen.	ὄντ-ος	οὔσ-ης	ὄντ-ος
dat.	ὄντ-ι	οὔσ-ῃ	ὄντ-ι

pl.

	masc.	**fem.**	**neut.**
nom.	ὄντ-ες	οὖσ-αι	ὄντ-α
acc.	ὄντ-ας	οὔσ-ας	ὄντ-α
gen.	ὄντ-ων	οὐσ-ῶν	ὄντ-ων
dat.	οὖσι(ν)	οὔσ-αις	οὖσι(ν)

παύ-ων, παύ-ουσα, παῦ-ον (παυοντ-), *stopping*

sing.

	masc.	**fem.**	**neut.**
nom.	παύ-ων	παύ-ουσ-α	παῦ-ον
acc.	παύ-οντ-α	παύ-ουσ-αν	παῦ-ον
gen.	παύ-οντ-ος	παυ-ούσ-ης	παύ-οντ-ος
dat.	παύ-οντ-ι	παυ-ούσ-ῃ	παύ-οντ-ι

pl.

	masc.	**fem.**	**neut.**
nom.	παύ-οντ-ες	παύ-ουσ-αι	παύ-οντ-α
acc.	παύ-οντ-ας	παυ-ούσ-ας	παύ-οντ-α
gen.	παυ-όντ-ων	παυ-ουσ-ῶν	παυ-όντ-ων
dat.	παύ-ουσι(ν)	παυ-ούσ-αις	παύ-ουσι(ν)

Note 1 ὤν, οὖσα, ὄν (ὀντ-) and παύων, παύουσα, παῦον (παυοντ-), like all active participles, follow the same '313' pattern of declension as πᾶς, πᾶσα, τᾶν (παντ-).

Present active participles of contract verbs

The way in which contract verbs form their participles is set out at *G&E*, pp. 83–4 §91. Below are the participles of active contract verbs laid out in full.

ποιέ-ων ουσα ον (οντ-) contracts to:
ποιῶν, ποιοῦσα, ποιοῦν (ποιουντ-), *making, doing*

sing.

	masc.	fem.	neut.
nom.	ποιῶν	ποιοῦσ-α	ποιοῦν
acc.	ποιοῦντ-α	ποιοῦσ-αν	ποιοῦν
gen.	ποιοῦντ-ος	ποιούσ-ης	ποιοῦντ-ος
dat.	ποιοῦντ-ι	ποιοῦσ-ῃ	ποιοῦντ-ι

pl.

	masc.	fem.	neut.
nom.	ποιοῦντ-ες	ποιοῦσ-αι	ποιοῦντ-α
acc.	ποιοῦντ-ας	ποιούσ-ας	ποιοῦντ-α
gen.	ποιούντ-ων	ποιουσ-ῶν	ποιούντ-ων
dat.	ποιοῦσι(ν)	ποιούσ-αις	ποιοῦσι(ν)

τιμά-ων ουσα ον (οντ-) contracts to:
τιμῶν, τιμῶσα, τιμῶν (τιμωντ-), *honouring*

sing.

	masc.	fem.	neut.
nom.	τιμῶν	τιμῶσ-α	τιμῶν
acc.	τιμῶντ-α	τιμῶσ-αν	τιμῶν
gen.	τιμῶντ-ος	τιμώσ-ης	τιμῶντ-ος
dat.	τιμῶντ-ι	τιμώσ-ῃ	τιμῶντ-ι

pl.

	masc.	fem.	neut.
nom.	τιμῶντ-ες	τιμῶσ-αι	τιμῶντ-α
acc.	τιμῶντ-ας	τιμώσ-ας	τιμῶντ-α
gen.	τιμώντ-ων	τιμωσ-ῶν	τιμώντ-ων
dat.	τιμῶσι(ν)	τιμώσ-αις	τιμῶσι(ν)

δηλό-ων ουσα ον (οντ-) contracts to:
δηλῶν, δηλοῦσα, δηλοῦν (δηλουντ-), ***showing, revealing***

sing.

	masc.	**fem.**	**neut.**
nom.	δηλῶν	δηλοῦσ-α	δηλοῦν
acc.	δηλοῦντ-α	δηλοῦσ-αν	δηλοῦν
gen.	δηλοῦντ-ος	δηλούσ-ης	δηλοῦντ-ος
dat.	δηλοῦντ-ι	δηλούσ-ῃ	δηλοῦντ-ι

pl.

	masc.	**fem.**	**neut.**
nom.	δηλοῦντ-ες	δηλοῦσ-αι	δηλοῦντ-α
acc.	δηλοῦντ-ας	δηλούσ-ας	δηλοῦντ-α
gen.	δηλούντ-ων	δηλουσ-ῶν	δηλούντ-ων
dat.	δηλοῦσι(ν)	δηλούσ-αις	δηλοῦσι(ν)

Present middle participles

παυ-όμεν-ος η ον, *stopping*

sing.

	masc.	**fem.**	**neut.**
nom.	παυ-όμεν-ος	παυ-ομέν-η	παυ-όμεν-ον
acc.	παυ-όμεν-ον	παυ-ομέν-ην	παυ-όμεν-ον
gen.	παυ-ομέν-ου	παυ-ομέν-ης	παυ-ομέν-ου
dat.	παυ-ομέν-ῳ	παυ-ομέν-ῃ	παυ-ομέν-ῳ

pl.

	masc.	**fem.**	**neut.**
nom.	παυ-όμεν-οι	παυ-όμεν-αι	παυ-όμεν-α
acc.	παυ-ομέν-ους	παυ-ομέν-ας	παυ-όμεν-α
gen.	παυ-ομέν-ων	παυ-ομέν-ων	παυ-ομέν-ων
dat.	παυ-ομέν-οις	παυ-ομέν-αις	παυ-ομέν-οις

Note 1 All middle participles are declined in the same way as καλ-ός ή όν.

Note 2 The participles of middle contract verbs are formed in the following way:
φοβε-όμεν-ος η ον contracts to φοβούμεν-ος η ον, *fearing*
θεα-όμενος η ον contracts to θεώμεν-ος η ον, *watching*
δηλο-όμεν-ος η ον on contracts to δηλούμεν-ος η ον, *showing, revealing*

First aorist active participles†

παύσ-ας, παύσ-ασ-α, παῦσ-αν (παυσ-αντ-), ***stopping, on stopping, having stopped***

sing.

	masc.	**fem.**	**neut.**
nom.	παύσ-ας	παύσ-ασ-α	παῦσ-αν
acc.	παύσ-αντ-α	παύσ-ασ-αν	παῦσ-αν
gen.	παύσ-αντ-ος	παυσ-άσ-ης	παύσ-αντ-ος
dat.	παύσ-αντ-ι	παυσ-άσ-ῃ	παύσ-αντ-ι

pl.

	masc.	**fem.**	**neut.**
nom.	παύσ-αντ-ες	παύσ-ασ-αι	παύσ-αντ-α
acc.	παύσ-αντ-ας	παυσ-άσ-ας	παύσ-αντ-α
gen.	παυσ-άντ-ων	παυσ-ασ-ῶν	παυσ-άντ-ων
dat.	παύσ-ασι(ν)	παυσ-άσ-αις	παύσ-ασι(ν)

Note 1 Like all active participles, first aorist active participles follow a '313' pattern of declension.

First aorist middle participles†

παυσ-άμεν-ος η ον, ***having stopped, on stopping, stopping***

sing.

	masc.	**fem.**	**neut.**
nom.	παυσ-άμεν-ος	παυσ-αμέν-η	παυσ-άμεν-ον
acc.	παυσ-άμεν-ον	παυσ-αμέν-ην	παυσ-άμεν-ον
gen.	παυσ-αμέν-ου	παυσ-αμέν-ης	παυσ-αμέν-ου
dat.	παυσ-αμέν-ῳ	παυσ-αμέν-ῃ	παυσ-αμέν-ῳ

pl.

	masc.	**fem.**	**neut.**
nom.	παυσ-άμεν-οι	παυσ-άμεν-αι	παυσ-άμεν-α
acc.	παυσ-αμέν-ους	παυσ-αμέν-ας	παυσ-άμεν-α
gen.	παυσ-αμέν-ων	παυσ-αμεν-ῶν	παυσ-αμέν-ων
dat.	παυσ-αμέν-οις	παυσ-αμέν-αις	παυσ-αμέν-οις

Note 1 Like all middle participles, first aorist middle participles are declined in the same way as καλ-ός ή όν.

Second aorist active participles†

λαβ-ών λαβ-οῦσα, λαβ-όν (λαβ-οντ-), *having taken, on taking, taking* (from λαμβάνω)

sing.

	masc.	**fem.**	**neut.**
nom.	λαβ-ών	λαβ-οῦσ-α	λαβ-όν
acc.	λαβ-όντ-α	λαβ-οῦσ-αν	λαβ-όν
gen.	λαβ-όντ-ος	λαβ-ούσ-ης	λαβ-όντ-ος
dat.	λαβ-όντ-ι	λαβ-ούσ-ῃ	λαβ-όντ-ι

pl.

	masc.	**fem.**	**neut.**
nom.	λαβ-όντ-ες	λαβ-οῦσ-αι	λαβ-όντ-α
acc.	λαβ-όντ-ας	λαβ-ούσ-ας	λαβ-όντ-α
gen.	λαβ-όντ-ων	λαβ-ουσ-ῶν	λαβ-όντ-ων
dat.	λαβ-οῦσι(ν)	λαβ-ούσ-αις	λαβ-οῦσι(ν)

Note 1 Like all active participles, second aorist active participles follow a '313' pattern of declension.

Second aorist middle participles†

γεν-όμεν-ος, γεν-ομέν-η, γεν-όμεν-ον, *having become, on becoming, becoming* (from γίγνομαι)

sing.

	masc.	**fem.**	**neut.**
nom.	γεν-όμεν-ος	γεν-ομέν-η	γεν-όμεν-ον
acc.	γεν-όμεν-ον	γεν-ομέν-ην	γεν-όμεν-ον
gen.	γεν-ομέν-ου	γεν-ομέν-ης	γεν-ομέν-ου
dat.	γεν-ομέν-ῳ	γεν-ομέν-ῃ	γεν-ομέν-ῳ

pl.

	masc.	**fem.**	**neut.**
nom.	γεν-όμεν-οι	γεν-όμεν-αι	γεν-όμεν-α
acc.	γεν-ομέν-ους	γεν-ομέν-ας	γεν-όμεν-α
gen.	γεν-ομέν-ων	γεν-ομέν-ων	γεν-ομέν-ων
dat.	γεν-ομέν-οις	γεν-ομέν-αις	γεν-ομέν-οις

Note 1 Like all middle participles, second aorist middle participles are declined in the same way as καλ-ός ή όν.

Root aorist participles†

βάς, βᾶσα, βάν (βαντ-), ***having gone, on going, going*** **(from βαίνω)**

sing.

	masc.	fem.	neut.
nom.	βάς	βᾶσ-α	βάν
acc.	βάντ-α	βᾶσ-αν	βάν
gen.	βαντ-ός	βάσ-ης	βαντ-ός
dat.	βαντ-ί	βάσ-ῃ	βαντ-ί

pl.

	masc.	fem.	neut.
nom.	βάντ-ες	βᾶσ-αι	βάντ-α
acc.	βάντ-ας	βάσ-ας	βάντ-α
gen.	βάντ-ων	βασ-ῶν	βάντ-ων
dat.	βᾶσι(ν)	βάσ-αις	βᾶσι(ν)

Note 1 Like all active participles, root aorist active participles follow a '313' pattern of declension.

γνούς, γνοῦσα, γνόν (γνοντ-)†**,** ***having realised, on realising, realising*** **(from γιγνώσκω)**

sing.

	masc.	fem.	neut.
nom.	γνούς	γνοῦσ-α	γνόν
acc.	γνόντ-α	γνοῦσ-αν	γνόν
gen.	γνοντ-ός	γνούσ-ης	γνοντ-ός
dat.	γνοντ-ί	γνούσ-ῃ	γνοντ-ί

pl.

	masc.	fem.	neut.
nom.	γνόντ-ες	γνοῦσ-αι	γνόντ-α
acc.	γνόντ-ας	γνούσ-ας	γνόντ-α
gen.	γνόντ-ων	γνουσ-ῶν	γνόντ-ων
dat.	γνοῦσι(ν)	γνούσ-αις	γνοῦσι(ν)

Adverbs

Formation of adverbs

Most adjectives may be turned into adverbs by changing the genitive plural -ων into -ως. Thus:

adjective	genitive plural	adverb
καλ-ός ή όν, *beautiful*	καλῶν	καλῶς, *beautifully*
δειν-ός ή όν, *terrible*	δεινῶν	δεινῶς, *terribly*

The following neuter forms of adjectives are commonly used adverbially.

πολύ, πολλά, *much, a lot*

μέγα (also μεγάλως), *greatly*

Note also the following common adverbs.

ἅμα, *at the same time*

ἄνω, *above*

εὖ, *well*

μάλιστα, *especially, particularly*

νῦν, *now*

πάνυ, *very, very much*

τέλος, *in the end, finally*

*Comparative and superlative adverbs**

Comparative adverbs are identical in appearance to the *neuter singular nominative* form of the comparative adjective. This rule applies to *all* adjectives, regular and irregular. Thus:

σοφώτερον, *more wisely*

δεινότερον, *more cleverly*

εὐφρονέστερον, *in a more well-disposed way*

ἄμεινον, *better* (as adverb)

κάκιον, *worse* (as adverb)

Superlative adverbs are identical in appearance to the *neuter plural nominative* form of the superlative adjective. This rule applies to *all* adjectives, regular and irregular. Thus:

σοφώτατα, *most wisely*

δεινότατα, *most cleverly*

εὐφρονέστατα, *in the most well-disposed way*

ἄριστα, *best* (as adverb)

κάκιστα, *worst* (as adverb)

Prepositions

The following is a list of all the prepositions met in Sections 1–9 of *G&E*.

ἀπό	+ gen.	*from, away from*
διά	+ acc. + gen.†	*because of* *through*
ἐγγύς	+ gen.	*near*
εἰς	+ acc.	*to, into, onto*
ἐκ(ἐξ)	+ gen.	*out of*
ἐν	+ dat.	*in*
ἐναντίον†	+ gen.	*opposite, in front of*
ἕνεκα†	+ gen.	*because, for the sake of*
ἐπί	+ acc. + gen.† + dat.†	*against, to* *on* *on, for the purpose of*
κατά	+ acc.	*in, on, by, according to*
μά*	+ acc.	*(no) by ...*
μετά	+ acc.† + gen.†	*after* *(in company) with*
νή*	+ acc.	*(yes) by ...*
παρά	+ acc. + gen † + dat.†	*along, alongside* *from* *with, near*
περί	+ acc. + gen.†	*about* *about, concerning*
πλήν†	+ gen.	*except*
πλησίον†	+ gen.	*near*
πρός	+ acc. + gen.† + dat.†	*towards* *in the name of, under the protection of* *near, in addition to*
σύν†	+ dat.	*with (the help of)*
ὑπέρ†	+ gen.	*for, on behalf of*
ὑπό†	+ gen.	*by, at the hands of*

Note 1 Properly, ἐγγύς, ἐναντίον and πλησίον are adverbs. Followed by the genitive, though, they mean 'near'.

3 Cases and their uses

Greek nouns are found in one of five cases: nominative, accusative, genitive, dative and vocative.

The nominative case

The case of the subject:

ὁ Ζηνόθεμις μένει.
Zenothemis waits.

τὸν Παρθενῶνα ὁρᾷ ὁ Ζηνόθεμις.
Zenothemis sees the Parthenon.

Other uses of the nominative case

- The case of the subject complement:

  ὁ Σωκράτης ἐστι φιλόσοφος.
  Socrates is a philosopher.

  ὁ Σωκράτης ἐστι καλός (or just ὁ Σωκράτης καλός).
  Socrates is beautiful.

  Note that a subject complement (and not a direct object) is used after 'linking' verbs such as *be* (εἰμί), *become* (γίγνομαι) and *seem* (δοκέω† and φαίνομαι).

The accusative case

The case of the direct object:

τὸν Παρθενῶνα ὁρᾷ ὁ Ζηνόθεμις.
Zenothemis sees the Parthenon.

ὁ Δικαιόπολις τὴν ἀκρόπολιν ὁρᾷ.
Dikaiopolis sees the Acropolis.

NB Not all verbs take direct objects. Those that do are called 'transitive' verbs. Verbs that do **not** take direct objects are called '*in*transitive' verbs, e.g. *come/go* (βαίνω, ἔρχομαι) and *wait* (μένω).

Note that some verbs can take two direct objects:

ὁ Σωκράτης με διδάσκει τὴν φιλοσοφίαν.
Socrates teaches me philosophy.

τοῦτο ἠρώτησα τὸν Σωκράτη.
I asked Socrates this.

Examples of verbs which can take two direct objects are *teach* (διδάσκω), *ask* (ἐρωτάω), *ask for* (αἰτέω†), *question* (ἐξετάζω†); *do someone good/ill* (καλὰ/κακὰ ποιέω*)

Other uses of the accusative case

- The case of the object complement:

  ὁ ῥαψῳδὸς τὸν λόγον καλὸν ποιεῖ.
  The rhapsode makes the story beautiful.

  τὸν Σωκράτη φιλόσοφον καλοῦσιν.
  They call Socrates a philosopher.

  This use is only found with certain verbs, e.g. *call* (καλέω), *make* (ποιέω), *consider* (ἡγέομαι†), *think* (νομίζω†, οἶμαι†) and *show* (δηλόω).

  For more on this sentence pattern, see p. 85 below.

- The 'cognate' accusative is a particular version of the direct object, in which the meaning of the verb and the object are related:

  θυσίας πολλὰς θύομεν.
  We make many sacrifices.
  (lit. *we sacrifice many sacrifices.*)

- To express length of time or space:†

  πέντε ἡμέρας ἔμενον.
  I waited for five days.

  ἡ πόλις ἀπέχει δέκα στάδια.
  The city is ten stades away.
  (A stade is about 185 metres, the length of a Greek athletics stadium.)

- Accusative of respect:

  σιωπῶ τὴν νίκην.
  I am saying nothing about the victory
  (lit. *I am silent in respect of the victory*).

  πόδας ὠκὺς Ἀχιλλεύς
  Swift-footed Achilles
  (lit. *swift* (ὠκὺς) *with respect to his feet* (πόδας))

  τί, *why*?, is also an accusative of respect, literally meaning 'with respect to what thing?'

- Note, too, the so-called 'internal accusative', when a neuter adjective is used in place of an adverb:

  μέγα βοᾷ.
  He shouts loudly (lit. *he shouts a big one* (i.e. shout)).
  (μέγα here is neuter singular accusative.)

- The accusative is also found with certain prepositions, often (but not always) expressing the idea of motion towards.

διὰ τὸν πόλεμον	***because of*** *the war*
εἰς τὸ πλοῖον	***to/onto*** *the ship*
ἐπὶ τοὺς Πέρσας	***against*** *the Persians*
κατὰ τὸν νόμον	***according to*** *the law*
*μὰ τὸν Δία	***no, by*** *Zeus*
†μετὰ ταῦτα	***after*** *these things* (*afterwards*)
*νὴ τὸν Ποσειδῶνα	***yes, by*** *Poseidon*
παρὰ τὸν ποταμόν	***along*** *the river*
περὶ τὴν νῆσον	***about*** *the island*
πρὸς τὸν Πειραιᾶ	***to/towards*** *the Piraeus*

The genitive case

The 'of' case:

τὸ τοῦ Ἡγεστράτου πλοῖον
the ship of Hegestratos (or, more naturally in English, *Hegestratos' ship*)

ὀλίγοι τῶν ναυτῶν
few of the sailors

στρατιὰ πολίτων
an army of citizens

φόβος τῶν Περσῶν
fear of the Persians

Note that the Greek genitive, like the English word 'of', covers a range of meanings:

- ownership or possession (*the ship of Hegestratos*)
- part of something (*few of the sailors*: the 'partitive' genitive)
- content or material (*an army of citizens*; *a crown of roses*)
- 'subjective' genitive (the *fear of the Persians towards the Athenians*; here it is the Persians who are afraid)
- 'objective' genitive (*the Athenians' fear of the Persians*; i.e. the Persians are the object of the Athenians' fear).

Other uses of the genitive case

- With some verbs, where English uses a direct object:

  ἀκούω τοῦ Ἡγεστράτου.
  I hear Hegestratos.

  ὁ ῥήτωρ τῶν πολίτων ἐκράτει.
  The speaker used to hold sway over the citizens.

  The following verbs take the genitive case:

ἀκούω†	*hear, listen to* (+ gen. of source of sound) Thus: ἀκούω τὸν ψόφον (acc.), *I hear the noise.* But: ἀκούω τοῦ ναύτου (gen.), *I hear the sailor.*
ἄρχομαι†	*begin*
ἄρχω*/βασιλεύω*	*rule*
γραφὴν γράφομαι*	*indict X* (acc.) *on a charge of Y* (gen.)
καταδικάζω*	*condemn/convict X* (gen.) *of Y* (acc.)
κρατέω	*hold sway/power over*
λαμβάνομαι†	*take hold of*
παύομαι	*cease from*
τυγχάνω†	*hit, chance on, happen on, be subject to*

- With certain adjectives:

  αἴτιος κακῶν
  responsible for disasters

  ἄξιος† τιμῆς
  worthy of honour

  πλέως† φόβου
  full of fear

- To express a comparison:†

  ὁ Σωκράτης σοφώτερός ἐστι τοῦ Στρεψιάδου.
  Socrates is wiser than Strepsiades.

  (But note that comparisons may also be expressed by using ἤ ('than'), and by placing the second item being compared in the same case as the first: e.g., ὁ Σωκράτης σοφώτερός ἐστι ἤ ὁ Στρεψιάδης, *Socrates is wiser than Strepsiades.*)

- To express time within which:†

  οἱ ναῦται ἀπέθανον νυκτός.
  The sailors died during/in the course of the night.

  ὁ φιλόσοφος ἀφίξεται πέντε ἡμερῶν.
  The philosopher will arrive within five days.

- To make an exclamation:

  φεῦ φεῦ τῶν Ἑλλήνων.
  Alas, alas for the Greeks!

- With certain prepositions:

ἀπὸ του λιμένος	***away from** the harbour*
†διὰ τῆς πόλεως	***through** the city*
ἐκ τῆς οἰκίας	***out of/from** the house*
†ἐπὶ τοῦ ἵππου	***on** the horse*
τῆς εἰρήνης ἕνεκα†	***for the sake of** peace* (ἕνεκα comes after the noun)
†μετὰ τῶν γερόντων	***(in company) with** the old men*
†παρὰ τοῦ μαθητοῦ	***from** the student*
†περὶ τῶν δίκων	***about** the lawsuits*
†πλὴν τῶν ναύτων	***except** the sailors*
†ὑπὲρ τῆς γυναικός	***for/on behalf of** the woman*
†ὑπὸ τοῦ γεωργοῦ	***by/at the hands** of the farmer*

- With certain adverbs when these are used as prepositions:

ἐγγὺς τοῦ ἄστεως	***near** the city*
†ἐναντίον τοῦ πλοίου	***opposite** the ship*
†πλησίον τῆς θύρας	***near** the door*

The dative case

1 The 'to' or 'for' case:

παρέχω τὰ χρήματα τῷ Ἡγεστράτῳ.
I give the money to Hegestratos.

ὁ ῥαψωδὸς τὸν λόγον τοῖς ναύταις ἔλεγεν.
The rhapsode was telling the story to the sailors.

οἱ παῖδες τὰ χρήματα τῷ πατρὶ ἔκλεψαν.
The children stole the money for their father.

NB When used in this way, the noun in the dative is generally animate, i.e. a living thing.

Or

2 The 'with' case†:

ὁ διδάσκαλος τοὺς μαθητὰς καλοῖς λόγοις ἐπαινεῖ.
The teacher praises his students with fine words.

τοὺς πολεμίους ἐμαχεσάμεθα ταῖς ἡμετέραις ναυσίν.
We fought the enemy with our ships.

ἀπέκρινε πολλῇ σπουδῇ.
He answered with much enthusiam.

NB When used in this way, the noun in the dative is generally inanimate, i.e. not a living thing.

1 The 'to' or 'for' use of the dative is usually reserved for a person who has some interest in an action or situation, or who receives some advantage from it. It is especially common after verbs which contain the idea of ***giving*** (e.g. παρέχω†) or ***saying*** (e.g. λέγω), where it is known as an **indirect object**:

παρέχω τὸν ἵππον τῷ βαρβάρῳ.
I am giving the horse (direct object) *to the foreigner* (indirect object).

εἰπέ τί μοι.
Say something to me!

Note that, in English, if the indirect object precedes a direct object, the word 'to' is omitted. For example, the last two sentences can be translated:

I am giving the foreigner the horse.
Tell me something!

Be careful not to confuse this use of English 'to' with 'to' indicating motion towards. Greek expresses the latter by using a preposition:

βαίνω πρὸς τὴν οἰκίαν.
I am going to the house.

2 The 'with' use of the dative identifies the ***instrument*** *with which*, the ***means*** *by which*, or the ***manner*** *in which* something is done.†

Instrument

ἀπέκτεινον αὐτὸν λίθῳ.
They killed him with a stone.

Here the dative indicates the ***instrument*** *with which* the killing took place.

Means

νόσῳ ἀπέθανεν.
He died through disease (i.e. *because of disease*).

Here the dative indicates the ***means*** *by which* the person died.

Manner

τὰ χρήματα ἐζήτουν πολλῇ σπουδῇ.
They were looking for the money with much enthusiasm.

Here the dative describes the ***manner*** *in which* the looking took place.

Manner can be expressed in English in a variety of ways, so you may need to be flexible when translating. For example:

ἀπέβαινε σιγῇ.
He departed in silence (or: *silently*).

Note that when an action is done *by a person*, Greek normally uses ὑπό plus the genitive case. Thus λίθῳ ἐβαλλόμην, *I was hit by a stone*; but ὑπὸ τοῦ Ἡγεστράτου ἐβαλλόμην, *I was hit by Hegestratos.*

Be careful in English to distinguish the instrumental meaning of 'with' from 'with' meaning 'in the company of':

Instrument

ἀπέκτεινον αὐτὸν λίθῳ.
They killed him with a stone.

Accompaniment

ἔρχονται μετὰ τοῦ Σωκράτους.
They are coming with Socrates (i.e. *in the company of Socrates*).

Other uses of the dative case

- With the verb *to be* (εἰμί) to express possession:†

  ἵππος μοι ἐστίν.
  I have a horse (lit. *there is a horse to me*).

  τῷ δεσπότῃ πολλοὶ δοῦλοι εἰσίν.
  The master has many slaves (lit. *there are many slaves to the master*).

- With some verbs, where English uses a direct object:

  οἱ Ἀθηναῖοι οὐ βοηθοῦσι τοῖς Λακεδαιμονίοις.
  The Athenians do not help the Spartans.

  τέλος ὁ νεανίας τῷ πατρὶ πείθεται.
  The young man finally obeys his father.

  The following verbs take the dative case:

βοηθέω	*help*
ἐμπίπτω*	*fall on, attack*
ἐντυγχάνω†	*I meet with*
ἕπομαι†	*follow*
ἥδομαι†	*enjoy, be pleased with*
ἡγέομαι†	*lead*
πάρειμι†	*be at hand, be present*
πείθομαι	*obey*
τιμάω	*fine*
χράομαι†	*use*

  (NB When τιμάω means *honour*, *value*, *reckon*, it is followed by a direct object in the accusative case.)

- With certain impersonal verbs:†

  ἀνάγκη ἐστὶ ταῖς γυναιξὶ εἰς το ἱερὸν ἰέναι.
  It is necessary for the women to go to the sanctuary.
  (NB The accusative can also be used with ἀνάγκη ἐστί: τὰς γυναῖκας.)

  δοκεῖ τοῖς Ἀθηναίοις πόλεμον ποιεῖσθαι.
  It seems a good idea to the Athenians to make war.
  (or: *The Athenians resolve/decide to make war.*)

  ἔξεστί μοι τὴν ἀκρόπολιν ὁρᾶν.
  It is possible for me to see the acropolis.

- With certain adjectives:

  †ὅμοιος ἡμῖν
  similar to us

  φίλη σοι
  friendly to you

- Expressing time when:†

  ἀφίξετο ὁ νεανίας ἐκείνῃ τῇ ἡμέρᾳ.
  The young man arrived on that day.

  πάντες οἱ ξένοι μίᾳ νυκτί ἀπέθανον.
  All the foreigners died in one night.

- With certain prepositions:

ἐν τῷ λιμένι	***in*** *the harbour*
†ἐπὶ νηΐ	***on*** *the ship*
†παρὰ τῷ βασιλεῖ	***with/near*** *the king*
†πρὸς τῷ ἱερῷ	***near*** *the sanctuary*
†πρὸς τούτοις	***in addition to this*** *(lit. these things)*
†σύν τῷ δεσπότῳ	***with (the help of)*** *the master*

The vocative case

The case used when a person or thing is directly addressed:

μὴ φρόντιζε, Ζηνόθεμι.
Don't worry, Zenothemis!

The vocative may be introduced by ὦ:

μὴ φρόντιζε, ὦ Ζηνόθεμι.
Don't worry, (O) Zenothemis!

ὦ πόλι, πόλι.
O city, city!

4 Sentence structure

Clauses

Every sentence contains at least one clause. A clause can consist of a small number of elements, but as a minimum will include a subject and a verb. Bear in mind that in Greek the subject may be embodied in the ending of the verb; e.g. βαίνεις, *you go*.

Clauses fall into a small number of patterns of which the following are the most common:

> subject + verb + direct object: *The dog chases the cat.*
>
> subject + verb: *The flower wilts.*
>
> subject + verb + subject complement: *Socrates is wise.*
>
> subject + verb + direct object + object complement: *Dikaiopolis considers Socrates wise.*

The choice of verb largely determines the shape of the clause:

- *Transitive* verbs such as 'chase' require a direct object.
- *Intransitive* verbs such as 'wilt' ***cannot*** take a direct object.
- 'Linking' verbs ('be', 'become','seem') need a subject complement.

Note that some verbs can be used both transitively (i.e. with a direct object) and intransitively (i.e. without a direct object):

He eats (transitive) *a five-course meal.*
He eats (intransitive) *at seven o'clock every evening.*

Some verbs, notably those expressing the idea of *giving*, *telling*, or *showing*, require an indirect object as well:

I give the book to Socrates.

A few verbs, generally the same as in English, might also require a prepositional phrase to complete the sense.

Socrates puts the book on the table.

Modification

A main clause contains all the ingredients needed to form a complete sentence. In practice, a series of these elementary sentences would be exceedingly dull, and most clauses tend to be expanded through the addition of other words, phrases and entire clauses, in a process known as *modification*.

A noun, for instance, can be modified by an adjective:

ὁ λιμήν	→	ὁ καλὸς λιμήν
the harbour	→	*the beautiful harbour*

Here the adjective 'beautiful' modifies or qualifies the noun 'harbour'. The reference is no longer just to 'the harbour', but specifically to 'the *beautiful* harbour'.

This section contains the basics of modification, the main device for extending a clause beyond its bare essentials.

Modifying a noun

Here are some standard devices for modifying a noun in Greek.

A noun can be modified by:

- an adjective:

  ὁ καλὸς λιμήν
  the beautiful harbour

- a noun or phrase in the genitive case:

  ὁ τῶν Ἀθηναίων λιμήν
  the Athenians' harbour

- a prepositional phrase standing between the definite article and its noun (the 'sandwich' construction):

  ὁ ἐν τῷ νήσῳ λιμήν
  the harbour on the island

- a participial clause:

  ὁ λιμήν, πλέως ὢν θορύβου καὶ βοῶν
  the harbour, being full of commotion and shouts

- a relative clause (not covered in this module):*

  ὁ λιμήν, ὃς πλέως ἦν θορύβου καὶ βοῶν
  the harbour, which was full of commotion and shouts

Modifying a verb

Verbs can be modified by adverbs and other 'adverbial' devices.

βραδέως πλεῖ τὸ πλοῖον.
The ship sails slowly.

Here the adverb 'slowly' qualifies the verb, in this particular case providing information about the *manner* in which the sailing took place.

Here are some common mechanisms for modifying a verb.

A verb can be modified by:

- an adverb:

  βραδέως πλεῖ τὸ πλοῖον.
  The ship sails slowly.

- a prepositional phrase:

  πλεῖ τὸ πλοῖον πρὸς Βυζάντιον.
  The ship sails towards Byzantium.

- a noun in the dative case:

  ὁ κυβερνήτης πλεῖ πολλῇ σπουδῇ.
  The captain sails with much enthusiasm.

- a subordinate clause introduced by a subordinating conjunction like 'when' or 'if':

  ὁ κυβερνήτης πλεῖ ἐπειδὴ νύξ ἐστι.
  The captain sails when it is night.

Together these devices are known as 'adverbials', because they play the same role as an adverb.

Simple sentences

Leaving aside special cases such as 'Fire!' and 'No entry!' (sometimes known as 'minor sentences'), a sentence can be defined as a grammatical unit containing at least one clause. A sentence consisting of a single clause is known as a ***simple sentence***:

ὁ Δικαιόπολις διώκει τὸν Ἡγέστρατον.
Dikaiopolis chases Hegestratos.

Compound sentences

A ***compound sentence*** consists of two or more clauses joined by a 'coordinating conjunction' such as 'and' (καί), 'but' (ἀλλά, δέ) or 'or' (ἤ):

ὁ Δικαιόπολις διώκει τὸν Ἡγέστρατον καὶ ὁ Ἡγέστρατος φεύγει.
Dikaiopolis chases Hegestratos and Hegestratos flees.

In this example one clause is simply added to another using the conjunction 'and' (the term 'conjunction' comes from the Latin word 'to join'). Neither clause is dependent on the other; each has equal weight in the construction of the sentence, which means that the sentence contains two main clauses. It is this equality between clauses that distinguishes *co*ordination from *sub*ordination (explained below).

Complex sentences

It is also possible for one clause to be dependent upon, or 'subordinate' to, another clause in the same sentence:

ἐπειδὴ νύξ ἐστι, ὁ Δικαιόπολις διώκει τὸν Ἡγέστρατον.
When it is night, Dikaiopolis chases Hegestratos.

The second clause in this example could stand on its own as a complete sentence (*Dikaiopolis chases Hegestratos*). The first, however, could not (*When it is night ...*): it is incomplete without a main clause and can therefore be called a ***subordinate clause***.

Sentences with at least one main clause and one subordinate clause are known as ***complex sentences***. The use of the term 'complex' does not imply that the meaning of the sentence is complicated, or that the sentence must be long and convoluted. It just refers to the way the sentence is constructed. Equally, a *simple sentence* does not necessarily have a simple meaning.

Subordination using adverbial clauses

In the example above, the clause was introduced by a 'subordinating conjunction', ἐπειδή, *when*, which indicated the time at which the chasing took place. Other subordinating conjunctions you meet include:

ὅτε	*when*
ἐπεί	*after, since, when*
ἐπειδή	*when, since, because*
ὡς	*as*
ὅτι†	*because* (note that ὅτι can also mean '*that*'; see below)
εἰ	*if*
εἰ μή	*if not*, i.e. *unless*

Subordinating conjunctions provide an important clue that a subordinate clause is about to begin. In Greek these conjunctions are usually the first word in the clause which they introduce (but not always, and especially not in poetry).

These clauses are 'adverbial' in that they play the role of adverbs, as you can see by substituting them for an adverb or other 'adverbial' device:

Adverbial clauses

Dikaiopolis chases Hegestratos when it is night.
Dikaiopolis chases Hegestratos after the Spartans have departed.

Other 'adverbial' devices

Dikaiopolis chases Hegestratos all over Athens.
Dikaiopolis chases Hegestratos with a big stick.

Subordination using noun clauses

A clause can also play the role of a noun, by being 'embedded' inside another clause:

λέγει δύο λόγους.
He says two words.

λέγει ὅτι ὁ Σωκράτης σοφός ἐστιν.
He says that Socrates is wise.

In the first sentence, the direct object of λέγει is a noun in the accusative case (λόγους). In the second, the role of the object is played by a subordinate clause introduced by ὅτι (*that*).

Whereas subordinate clauses introduced by subordinating conjunctions behave like adverbs, embedded clauses play the role of nouns, and for that reason are sometimes called ***noun clauses***.

The two types of noun clause covered in this module are:

Indirect statements ('that' clauses)

ὁ Σωκράτης λέγει ὅτι οὐδὲν γιγνώσκει.
Socrates says that he knows nothing.

In such sentences ὡς may be used instead of ὅτι.

Indirect questions

ἐρωτῶ ποῦ ἐστιν ὁ Σωκράτης.
I ask where Socrates is.

In such sentences the question word in an indirect question is often changed to the indirect form (e.g. ποῦ becomes ὅπου). See Appendix 3 for a complete list.

A note on indirect statement

There are three ways in Greek to represent an indirect statement:

- As described above, a verb of saying (especially λέγω and εἶπον) followed by ὅτι or ὡς:

  ὁ Σωκράτης λέγει ὅτι καλός ἐστι ὁ Παρθενῶν.
  Socrates says that the Parthenon is beautiful.

- A verb of knowing (γιγνώσκω, οἶδα) or perceiving (ἀκούω, ὁράω) generally followed by a participle:

  ὁ Σωκράτης ὁρᾷ τὸν Παρθενῶνα καλὸν ὄντα.
  Socrates sees that the Parthenon is beautiful
  (lit. *Socrates sees the Parthenon being beautiful*).

(ὅτι or ὡς may also be used with these verbs; but if so, the implication is that the person 'knows' or 'perceives' the fact by hearsay rather than direct observation. Thus ὁ Σωκράτης οἶδε ὅτι καλός ἐστι ὁ Παρθενῶν would imply that Socrates knows that the Parthenon is beautiful because he has been told it is rather than because he has seen it for himself.)

- There is also the 'accusative and infinitive' construction, found with a range of verbs of saying (especially φημί) and thinking (e.g. νομίζω, οἶμαι):

  ὁ Σωκράτης νομίζει τὸν Παρθενῶνα καλὸν εἶναι.
  Socrates thinks the Parthenon to be beautiful (i.e. that the Parthenon is beautiful).

  ὁ Σωκράτης φησὶ τὸν Παρθενῶνα καλὸν εἶναι.

  Socrates says that the Parthenon is beautiful
  (lit. *Socrates says the Parthenon to be beautiful*).

Appendices

Appendix One: Augments

To change a Greek verb from the present into the aorist or imperfect tense, an augment must be added. There are two kinds of augment: if the verb stem begins with a consonant, an ἐ- is added (the technical name for this is a *syllabic* augment); if the verb stem begins with a vowel, then this vowel lengthens if it can (this is called a *temporal* augment). Thus:

α	lengthens to	η	ἄρχομαι	→	ἠρξάμην	*I began*
			ἀγαγ-	→	ἤγαγον	*I led*
ε	lengthens to	η[1]	ἐρωτάω	→	ἠρώτησα	*I asked*
			ἐλθ-	→	ἦλθον	*I went*
ο	lengthens to	ω	ὁμολογέω	→	ὡμολόγησα	*I agreed*
ι	lengthens to	ῑ	ἀφικ-	→	ἀφῑκόμην	*I arrived*
υ	lengthens to	ῡ	ὑβρίζω	→	ὕ̄βριζα	*I treated violently*
ω and η	remain unchanged (they are already long vowels)		ἡγέομαι	→	ἡγησάμην	*I led*
αυ/ευ	lengthens to	ηυ	εὑρ-	→	ηὗρον	*I found*
αι/ᾳ/ει	lengthens to	ῃ	αἰτέω (iota becomes subscript)	→	ᾔτησα	*I asked*
οι	lengthens to	ῳ	οἰκέω (iota becomes subscript)	→	ᾤκησα	*I dwelt*

[1] The first ἐ- of a handful of verbs lengthens to εἱ- (rather than ἠ). The only examples of such verbs met in *G&E* Sections 1–9 are ἕπομαι, *I follow*, and ἔχω, *I have* (in the imperfect only) and ἐάω, *I allow* (in the imperfect *and* aorist). Thus:
εἱπόμην, *I was following*
εἶχον, *I was having*
εἴων, *I was allowing*
εἴασα, *I allowed*

Compound verbs

When turning a present tense compound verb into the aorist, it must be borne in mind that it is the verb *stem* that must be augmented, not the whole verb. Therefore, the augment comes between the prefix and the main stem. Observe the following.

ἀποβαίνω	→	ἀπέβην
εἰσβαίνω	→	εἰσέβην
ἐκβαίνω	→	ἐξέβην
ἐμβαίνω	→	ἐνέβην
ἐπιβαίνω	→	ἐπέβην
καταβαίνω	→	κατέβην
προβαίνω	→	προέβην (or προὔβην)
μεταβαίνω	→	μετέβην
ἐγγράφω	→	ἐνέγραψα

Note 1 When the prefix ends in a vowel, this generally drops out, the exception being προ-. Note, too, that ἐκ- changes to ἐξ- before the augment.

Note 2 In compounds that include the element ἐν, the spelling of ἐν- is often modified in the present tense, depending on the consonant that follows: e.g. ἐν + βαίνω = ἐμβαίνω. Note the spelling of the aorist forms of such verbs in the list above, however, where ἐν- is always found in front of the augment (ε), e.g. ἐνέβην.

Appendix Two: Dative plurals of type 3a nouns

The dative plural of type 3a nouns is formed by adding the ending -σι or -σιν to the *stem* of the noun. (Like the movable ν on the end of certain verb forms, the ν is often used by authors either when the noun-form sits at the end of a sentence or clause, or when the following word in the sentence begins with a vowel.)

The σ of the -σι(ν) ending combines with the last consonant of the noun's *stem* in the predictable ways set out below.

Stems ending in λ or ϱ

For stems ending in ϱ (or λ) (*liquid* consonants, pronounced by running the tongue over the roof of the mouth above the teeth), add the -σι(ν) ending to the noun's stem.

ῥήτωρ (ῥητορ-), *orator*	ῥητορ + σι(ν)	→	ῥήτορσι(ν)

Stems ending in δ, ζ, θ or τ

With stems ending in δ, ζ, τ or θ (*dental* consonants, pronounced on the teeth), the final consonant drops out and is replaced by the σ. (Note below, though, different rules when the stem ends in κτ or ντ.)

παῖς (παιδ-), *child*	παιδ + σι(ν)	→	παισί(ν)
πατρίς (πατριδ-), *fatherland*	πατριδ + σι(ν)	→	πατρίσι(ν)
πούς (ποδ-), *foot*	ποδ + σι(ν)	→	ποσί(ν)

Stems ending in μ or ν

The same happens with stems ending in ν (or μ) (*nasal* consonants, pronounced through the nose): the final consonant drops out and is replaced by the σ.

γείτων (γειτον-), *neighbour*	γειτον + σι(ν)	→	γείτοσι(ν)
δαίμων (δαιμον-), *god*	δαιμον + σι(ν)	→	δαίμοσι(ν)
Ἕλλην (Ἑλλην-), *Greek*	Ἑλλην + σι(ν)	→	Ἕλλησι(ν)

Stems ending in γ, κ, χ and κτ

Stems ending in γ, κ or χ (*guttural* or *velar* consonants, pronounced in the throat) combine with -σι(ν) to produce -ξι(ν).

γυνή (γυναικ-), *woman*	γυναικ + σι(ν)	→	γυναιξί(ν)
κῆρυξ (κηρυκ-), *herald*	κηρυκ + σι(ν)	→	κήρυξι(ν)

The same happens with the stem-ending κτ: these consonants also combine with -σι(ν) to produce -ξι(ν).

νύξ (νυκτ-), *night*	νυκτ + σι(ν)	→	νυξί(ν)
ἄναξ (ἀνακτ-), *lord*	ἀνακτ + σι(ν)	→	ἄναξι(ν)

Stems ending in οντ

The stem-ending οντ combines with -σι(ν) to produce -ουσι(ν).

γέρων (γεροντ-), *old man*	γεροντ + σι(ν)	→	γερουσι(ν)

Exceptions: πατήρ, ἀνήρ and χείρ

Two exceptions to these rules come in the form of the slightly irregular nouns πατήρ (πατ(ε)ρ-), *father*, and ἀνήρ (ἀνδρ-), *man*, both of which form their dative plurals by adding -ασι(ν) to their (syncopated) stems (see p. 15 above).

πατήρ (πατ(ε)ρ-), *father*	πατράσι(ν)
ἀνήρ (ἀνδρ-), *man*	ἀνδράσι(ν)

The noun χείρ, *hand*, has a slightly irregular dative plural too.

χείρ (χειρ-), *hand*	χερσί(ν)

For information:

As you encounter only a small number of 3rd declension nouns in *G&E* Sections 1–9, there are two combinations of consonant plus -σι(ν) which are not represented by nouns met in the course of your A275 studies. The stems of other 3rd declension nouns combine with the -σι(ν) ending in the following ways.

Stems ending in β, π or φ

Stems ending in β, π or φ (*labial* consonants, pronounced on the lips) combine with the -σι(ν) ending to produce -ψι(ν).

φλέψ (φλεβ-), *vein*	φλεβ + σι(ν)	→	φλέψι(ν)

Stems ending in αντ

With stems ending in αντ, the two final consonants are replaced by the σ.

γίγας (γιγαντ-), *giant*	γιγαντ + σ	→	γίγασι(ν)

Appendix Three: Correlatives

On p. 109 §125 of *G&E*, you are introduced to 'correlatives' – words such as ποῦ, *where?*, and που, *somewhere*, which (as in English) share a common root. Below is a fuller list. Note that some of these forms are not met in *G&E* Sections 1–9 and are given **for information** only.

interrogative		**relative**	**demonstrative**	**indefinite**
direct	**indirect**			
τίς	ὅστις*, *who?*	ὅς*, *who*	οὗτος, ὅδε†, *this*	τις, *someone*
πόσος*	ὁπόσος†, *how great?*	ὁπόσος*, ὅσος, *as great as*	τοσοῦτος*, *so great*	ποσός *, *of a certain size*
πόσοι*	ὁπόσοι, *how many?*	ὁπόσοι*, ὅσοι*, *as many as*	τοσοῦτοι*, *so many*	ποσοί*, *of a certain number*
ποῖος*	ὁποῖος*, *of what kind?*	ὁποῖος*, οἷος*, *such as*	τοιοῦτος†, *such*	ποιός*, *of a certain kind*
ποῦ	ὅπου, *where?*	οὗ*, ὅπου, *where*	αὐτοῦ*, *here* ἐκεῖ*, ἐνθάδε*, *there*	που, *somewhere*
ποῖ	ὅποι*, *where to?*	οἷ*, ὅποι*, *to where*	ἐκεῖσε*, *to there*	ποι*, *to somewhere*
πόθεν	ὁπόθεν*, *where from?*	ὁπόθεν*, ὅθεν*, *from where*	ἐνθένδε*, *from here* ἐκεῖθεν*, *from there*	ποθέν*, *from somewhere*
πότε	ὁπότε, *when?*	ὅτε, *when*	τότε, *then*	ποτέ†, *sometime*
πῶς	ὅπως*, *how?*	ὅπως*, ὡς*, *as, in such a way*	οὕτω(ς), ὧδε*, *thus, in this way*	πως, *somehow, in some way*

Appendix Four: The middle voice

In Sections 1 and 2 of *G&E* you are introduced to two verbs which may be translated in the same way: βαίνω and ἔρχομαι, both of which signify *I come* or *I go*. There is, however, a fundamental difference in form between these two verbs: βαίνω is an active verb (and takes active endings), whereas ἔρχομαι is a middle verb (and takes middle endings). The two verbs are conjugated in the present tense in the following way.

	βαίνω, *I come/go*		**ἔρχομαι, *I come/go***
sing.	βαίν-ω	*I come/go*	ἔρχ-ομαι
	βαίν-εις	*you* (s.) *come/go*	ἔρχ-ῃ (-ει)
	βαίν-ει	*he/she/it comes/goes*	ἔρχ-εται
pl.	βαίν-ομεν	*we come/go*	ἐρχ-όμεθα
	βαίν-ετε	*you* (pl.) *come/go*	ἔρχ-εσθε
	βαίν-ουσι(ν)	*they come/go*	ἔρχ-ονται

βαίνω is an active verb and in the present tense will be found only with the active endings -ω, -εις, -ει, etc. Similarly a verb such as γιγνώσκω, *I know/recognise*, will be found only with active endings – neither verb has a middle form. ἔρχομαι, on the other hand, is a middle verb and in the present tense will be found only with middle endings -ομαι, -ῃ (-ει), -εται, etc. Verbs such as γίγνομαι, *I become*, and θεάομαι, *I watch*, are found only with middle endings, and neither of these verbs has an active form.

For the most part, then, it will be apparent when you learn a new verb whether it is active or middle depending on whether the first person singular form of the verb – the form you are asked to commit to memory – ends in -ω (like βαίνω) or -ομαι (like ἔρχομαι). However, some of the active verbs you learn are, on occasion, found with middle endings. For example, you will find both παύω and παύομαι, both meaning *I stop*, and ποιέω and ποιέομαι, both meaning *I make/do*. For such verbs, there is a difference either in nuance or meaning between their active and middle uses. The differences between these uses generally fall into one (or more) of three overlapping categories.

Category 1

The active form of the verb is used in a sentence where there is a direct object, the middle form in a sentence where there is no direct object.

Observe the following pairs of English sentences.

The pig is opening the door.	*The door is opening.*
The pig is closing the show.	*The show is closing tonight.*
The pig is stopping the traffic.	*The traffic is stopping.*

In the sentences on the left-hand side, the verbs are all followed by direct objects: the pig is variously opening *the door*; closing *the show*; and stopping *the traffic*. (When a verb is followed by a direct object it is called a 'transitive' verb.) In the sentences on the right, however, there is no direct object expressed (and the verbs are thus said to be '**in**transitive'). In Greek the verb παύω, *I stop*, is found in its ***active*** form when there is a direct object in the sentence, and in its middle form, παύομαι, when there is ***no*** direct object.

Observe the following.

active	**middle**
παύω τὸν ἄνθρωπον. *I stop the man.*	παύομαι τρέχων. *I stop running.*
ἔπαυσε τοὺς φύλακας. *He stopped the guards.*	ἐπαύσατο ἐν τῇ ἀγορᾷ. *He stopped in the agora.*

The authors of *G&E* are careful to observe this rule when using παύω/παύομαι. As you will discover, Greek authors themselves are not always as rigorous and sometimes use the active where the middle voice would be expected!

Category 2

The active form of the verb is used in a sentence where there is a direct object, whereas the middle form of the verb is used reflexively: i.e. to indicate that the subject is doing something *to* himself or herself.

Observe the following pairs of sentences.

active	**middle**
The farmer is washing the pig.	*The farmer is washing.*
The doctor is waking up her children.	*The doctor is waking up.*

In the sentences on the left, the action of the verb – washing, waking – is being performed on someone or something other than the subject of the verb – the pig and the children, respectively. In the sentences on the right, on the other hand, the opposite is true. The farmer isn't washing anyone else, rather he is washing *himself*; similarly, the doctor is waking no one else up but *herself*. Verbs used in this way are said to be *reflexive* – and one way in which the middle voice of some verbs is used in Greek is to display a reflexive action.

Observe the following use of the two verbs λούω, *I wash*, and ἐγείρω, *I wake up*.

active	**middle**
λούει τὸν ναύτην. *He is washing the sailor.*	ὁ ναύτης λούεται. *The sailor is washing (himself).*
ὁ βασιλεὺς ἐγείρει τὸν δοῦλον. *The king is waking up the slave.*	ὁ βασιλεὺς ἐγείρεται. *The king is waking up.*

Category 3

The middle form of a verb is used to indicate that the subject gains some particular benefit or advantage from performing the action of the verb (the so-called 'autobeneficial' use of the middle voice).

This use of the middle voice is probably the most difficult for English-speakers to grasp and for good reason, since it is sometimes impossible to capture in English idiom. With some verbs, such as ποιέω, *I do/make*, the difference between the active and middle uses is one of fine nuance.

active	middle
οἱ Ἀθηναῖοι ποιοῦσι καλοὺς λόγους. *The Athenians are making fine speeches.*	οἱ Ἀθηναῖοι ποιοῦνται σπονδάς. *The Athenians are making peace treaties.*

The difference between the active and middle uses resists translation in these instances. However, the implication in the sentence on the right is that the Athenians are benefiting from their actions in a way that they are not in the sentence on the left. In fact, the making of war and peace seems always to demand the middle voice, ποιέομαι, in Greek. With other activities it is interesting to observe how Greek authors use the two voices of this verb: it is not always in a way one might expect!

With other verbs there is a clearer distinction between the active and middle meanings. For example, the verb λύω in its active form means *I release* or *I ransom* (in the sense 'I gain money for releasing a hostage'). In its middle form, however, λύομαι, the verb means 'I gain someone's release (for money)' (and so, confusingly, may also be translated as *I ransom*, appealing to a different meaning of 'ransom' in English). Thus:

active	middle
λύω τὸν ξένον *I release the foreigner* (or 'ransom', i.e. charge for his release).	λύομαι τὸν ξένον *I ransom the foreigner* (i.e. gain his release for money).

Two more verbs you have met with distinct active and middle meanings are αἱρέω, *I take*, and αἱρέομαι, *I choose*; and φέρω, *I carry, bear, endure*, and φέρομαι, *I win*.

The middle voice is a conceptually complex, but none the less fascinating, area of Greek grammar. As with many areas of Greek, the best way to get to grips with it is to read as widely and observantly as possible and to observe how the Greek authors themselves make use of it.

Vocabulary lists

These vocabulary lists consist of the total 'Vocabulary to be learnt' for all sections of A275. **They will help you throughout the module and in your preparation for the examination**. When trying to memorise vocabulary, you should remember that 'little and often' is best.

For convenience of reference, the vocabulary is set out in two forms:

1 by section of *G&E*

2 alphabetically, in a consolidated vocabulary list, as in the 'Total Vocabulary' at the end of *G&E*.

Please note the following:

- Words marked with an asterisk (*) will ***not*** be tested **in any part** of the examination.
- Words marked with a dagger (†) in the consolidated vocabulary list only appear in the 'Vocabulary to be learnt' in Sections 7–9 of *Reading Greek*. These words will ***not*** appear unglossed (i.e. without a definition) in **Part 1** of the examination (the compulsory foundation-level language section). They may, however, appear in **Part 2** of the examination (the optional higher-level language section).

The different types of vocabulary are set out in the following ways:

- Verbs – only the first person singular is given. Contract verbs are given in their uncontracted form.
- Nouns – the genitive ending is supplied, as is the definite article which provides the gender.
- Adjectives – usually all the genders are given (in the nominative singular).

In the case of some entries in the *G&E* vocabulary, a simplified version is given here. If necessary you can consult the *G&E* 'Total Vocabulary' directly.

Section-by-section vocabulary list

Vocabulary for Section 1

ἀεί	always
ἀκούω	hear, listen to (+ gen. of person/thing) (+ acc. of sound)
ἀκριβῶς	accurately, closely
ἀκρόπολις -εως, ἡ	the Acropolis
ἀληθῆ -ῶν, τά	(neut. pl. of ἀληθής = true) the truth
ἀλλά	but
ἀναβαίνω	go up, come up
ἄνθρωπος -ου, ὁ	man, fellow
ἀπό	(+ gen.) from, away from
ἀποθνῄσκω	die
ἀποχωρέω	go away, depart
ἆρα;	? *indicates question*
ἄριστος-η-ον	best, very good
βαθέως	deeply
βαίνω	go, come, walk
βλέπω	look (at)
βοηθέω	(+ dat.) run to help, help
γάρ	for
γε	at least, at any rate
γῆ -ῆς, ἡ	land
γιγνώσκω	know, think, resolve
δέ	and, but
δεῦρο	here, over here
δῆλος-η-ον	clear, obvious
δηλόω	show, reveal
διὰ τί;	why?
διώκω	pursue
δύω	sink
ἐγώ	I
ἔγωγε	I at least, for my part
εἰμί	be (I am etc.)
εἰς	(+ acc.) to, into, onto
εἰσβαίνω	enter, board, go onto
ἐκ, ἐξ	(+ gen.) out of
*ἐλθέ (imperat. sing.)	come!
Ἕλλην -ηνος, ὁ	Greek
ἔμπειρος-ον	skilled, experienced
ἐμπόριον -ου, τό	market-place
ἐν	(+ dat.) in, on, among
ἔπειτα	then, next
ἔργον -ου, τό	task, job, work, duty
ἔχω	have, hold
ἤ	or
ἡμεῖς	we
ἡμέτερος-α-ον	our(s)
θάλαττα -ης, ἡ	sea
καί	and, also
κακός-ή-όν	bad, evil, mean, cowardly, lowly
κακῶς	badly, evilly
καλός-ή-όν	fine, beautiful, good
καλῶς	well, finely, beautifully
καταβαίνω	go down, come down
κυβερνήτης -ου, ὁ	captain, helmsman
λέγω	speak, say, tell, mean
*λέμβος -ου, ὁ	boat, life-boat
μέν ... δέ	on the one hand ... on the other hand
μένω	remain, wait for
μή	no, not, don't

μῶρος-α-ον	stupid, foolish
ναί	yes
ναῦς, νεώς, ἡ	ship
ναύτης -ου, ὁ	sailor
*νεώριον -ου, τό	dockyard
νῦν	now
ὁ ἡ τό	the
οἶδα	know
*οἴμοι	alas! oh dear!
ὁράω	see
ὅτι	that
οὐ, οὐκ, οὐχ	no, not
οὐδέν	nothing
οὖν	so, really, then, therefore
παίζω (πρός + acc.)	play, joke at
Παρθενών -ῶνος, ὁ	the Parthenon
περί	(+ acc.) about
πλέω	sail
πλοῖον -ου, τό	vessel, ship
ποῖ;	where to?
ποιέω	make, do
πολλά (neut. pl. of πολύς)	many things
ποῦ;	where?
πρός	(+ acc.) to, towards
πῶς γὰρ οὔ	of course
*ῥαψῳδός -οῦ, ὁ	rhapsode
ῥίπτω	throw
σαφῶς	clearly
σεαυτόν	yourself (sing.)
στρατηγός -οῦ, ὁ	general
σύ	you (sing.)
σῴζω	save, keep safe
σῶος-α-ον	safe
σωτηρία -ας, ἡ	safety, salvation
*τὰ ναυτικά	lit. 'the naval-things', naval matters
*τὰ στρατηγικά	lit. 'the leader's-things', leadership, generalship
*τὰ στρατιωτικά	lit. 'the soldier's-things', military matters
τε ... καί	both ... and
τί;	what?
τίς;	who?
ὑμεῖς	you (pl.)
φεύγω	run off, flee
φίλος -ου, ὁ	friend
φίλος-η-ον	dear, friendly, one's own
φροντίζω	think, worry
ὦ	O (when addressing someone, as in 'O Socrates')
ὡς	how!

Vocabulary for Section 2

ἀγαθός-ή-όν	good, noble
Ἀθηναῖος -ου, ὁ	Athenian
ἅμα	at the same time
ἀναχωρέω	retreat
ἀπορέω	be at a loss, have no resources
ἀπορία -ας, ἡ	perplexity, lack of provisions
αὖθις	again
βάρβαρος -ου, ὁ	barbarian, foreigner
βέβαιος-α-ον	secure
βοή -ῆς, ἡ	shout
βραδέως	slowly
γίγνομαι	become, be born, happen, arise
διά	(+ acc.) because of
διέρχομαι	go through, relate
δουλό-ομαι	enslave (for oneself)
ἐλευθερία -ας, ἡ	freedom
ἐλεύθερος-α-ον	free
ἐλευθερόω	set free
ἐμός-ή-όν	my, mine
ἐπειδή	when
ἐπέρχομαι	go against, attack
ἐπί	(+ acc.) at, against, to, to get
ἔρχομαι	go, come
ἡδέως	with pleasure, sweetly, happily
ἤδη	by now, now, already
ἡσυχάζω	be quiet, keep quiet
ἡσυχία -ας, ἡ	quiet, peace
θεά -ᾶς, ἡ	goddess
θεάομαι	observe, watch
κάλλιστος-η-ον	very fine, very good, most beautiful
λόγος -ου, ὁ	story, tale
μάχομαι	fight
ναυμαχία -ας, ἡ	naval battle
νικάω	conquer, win, defeat
νίκη -ης, ἡ	victory, conquest
*ὁμόνοια -ας, ἡ	agreement, harmony
ὅσος-η-ν	how great
οὐκέτι	no longer
οὕτω(ς)	thus, so; in this way
παρά	(+ acc.) along, beside
πίπτω	fall, die
πολέμιοι -ων, οἱ	the enemy
πολέμιος-α-ον	hostile, enemy
πόλεμος -ου, ὁ	war
πότερον ... ἤ	whether ... or
προσέρχομαι	advance, go/come towards
σιωπάω	be silent
σκοπέω	look at, consider, examine
στρατιά -ᾶς, ἡ	army
ταχέως	quickly
τέλος	in the end, finally
τι	a, something
τόλμα -ης, ἡ	daring
τολμάω	dare, be daring, undertake
φοβέομαι	fear, be afraid of, respect
ψευδῶς	falsely
ὥσπερ	like, as

Vocabulary for Section 3

ἄγε (imperat. sing.)	come!
ἀλλήλους	each other, one another
ἄλλος-η-ο	other, the rest of
ἀνήρ ἀνδρός, ὁ	man
ἀφικνέομαι	arrive, come
βοάω	shout (for)
*γείτων -ονος, ὁ	neighbour
δεινός-ή-όν	terrible, dire, clever
δή	then, indeed
ἐγγύς	(+ gen.) near, nearby
εἰπέ (imperat. sing.)	speak! tell me!
ἐκεῖνος-η-ο	that, (s)he, it
ἐμβαίνω	embark
ἐπειδή	when, since, because
ἐρωτάω	ask
ἔτι	still, yet
εὖ	well
εὐχή -ῆς, ἡ	prayer
εὔχομαι	pray
Ζεύς Διός, ὁ	Zeus
ζητέω	look for, seek
θεάομαι	watch, gaze at
θόρυβος -ου, ὁ	noise, din
θύρα -ας, ἡ	door
θυσία -ας, ἡ	sacrifice
θύω	sacrifice
ἰδού (imperat. sing.)	look! here! hey!
καθεύδω	sleep
καλέω	call, summon
κατά	(+ acc.) in, on, by, according to
*κελευστής -οῦ, ὁ	boatswain
κελεύω	order
κίνδυνος -ου, ὁ	danger
Λακεδαιμόνιος -ου, ὁ	Spartan
λαμβάνω	take, capture
*λαμπάς -άδος, ἡ	torch
λιμήν -ένος, ὁ	harbour
λόγος -ου, ὁ	word, speech, story, tale
μανθάνω	learn, understand
μέγας μεγάλη μέγα	great, big
ναυτικός-ή-όν	naval
νῆσος -ου, ἡ	island
νύξ, νυκτός, ἡ	night
οἴκαδε	homewards
οἰκία -ας, ἡ	house
οἴκοι	at home
ὅπλα -ων, τά	weapons, arms
οὐδέ	and not, not even
οὗτος αὕτη τοῦτο	this, (s)he, it
οὑτοσί αὑτηί τουτί	this here
παῖς παιδός, ὁ	slave, child
πατρίς -ίδος, ἡ	fatherland
πόθεν;	from where?
πολύς πολλή πολύ	much, many
πορεύομαι	march, journey, go
*πυρά -ῶν, τά	fire-signal
*σπένδω	pour a libation
σπεύδω	hurry
*σπονδή -ῆς, ἡ	libation
σωτήρ -ῆρος, ὁ	saviour
τέχνη -ης, ἡ	skill, art, expertise
τρέχω	run

*τριήραρχος -ου, ὁ	trierarch
φαίνομαι	appear, seem
χωρέω	go, come

Vocabulary for Section 4

ἀνομία -ας, ἡ	lawlessness
ἀπάγω	lead, take away
ἀποκτείνω	kill
ἀποφεύγω	escape, run off
*ἀσέβεια -ας, ἡ	irreverence to the gods
ἄστυ -εως, τό	city
*ἀτιμάζω	hold in dishonour, dishonour
αὐτόν-ήν-ό	him, her, it, (pl.) them
*ἀφέλκω	drag off
βασιλεύς -έως, ὁ	king
*βωμός -οῦ, ὁ	altar
γεωργός -οῦ, ὁ	farmer
γυνή γυναικός, ἡ	woman
*δαίμων -ονος, ὁ	god, daimon
δεσπότης -ου, ὁ	master
διαφθείρω	destroy, kill
δοῦλος -ου, ὁ	slave
*ἐπικαλέομαι	call upon (to witness)
ἔτι καὶ νῦν	even now, still now
εὔφρων-ον	well-disposed
θεός -οῦ, ὁ, ἡ	god(-dess)
θνητός-ή-όν	mortal
ἱερόν -οῦ, τό	sanctuary
*ἱκέτης -ου, ὁ	suppliant
*κακοδαίμων-ον	unlucky, dogged by an evil daimon
κῆρυξ -υκος, ὁ	herald
κρατέω	(+ gen.) hold sway/power over
κωλύω	prevent, stop
λανθάνω	escape notice of X (acc.) in –ing (part.)
*μά	(+ acc.) no, by ...! (e.g. μὰ Δία, no, by Zeus!)
μάλιστα	especially, particularly; yes
μισέω	hate
νεκρός -οῦ, ὁ	corpse
*νή	(+ acc.) yes, by ...! (e.g. νὴ Δία, yes, by Zeus!)
νόμος -ου, ὁ	law, convention
νόσος -ου, ἡ	illness, plague, disease
ξεῖνος / ξένος -ου, ὁ	foreigner, guest, host
οἴκησις -εως, ἡ	dwelling
ὀλίγος-η-ον	small, few
*ὀλοφύρομαι	lament, mourn for
ὀρθός-ή-όν	straight, correct, right
οὐδείς οὐδεμία οὐδέν	no; no one, nothing
πάσχω	suffer, experience, undergo
παύομαι	stop (+ part.)
πλῆθος -ους, τό	number, crowd, the people
πόλις -εως, ἡ	city, city-state
πρᾶγμα -ατος, τό	thing, matter, affair, (pl.) troubles
πρέσβεις -εων, οἱ	ambassadors
*πρεσβευτής -οῦ, ὁ	ambassador
*πυρά -ᾶς, ἡ	funeral pyre
*σκεύη -ων, τά	gear, furniture
*τάξις -εως, ἡ	battle-array, order, rank
τιμάω	honour
τις, τι	a, a certain (man etc.), someone, something
τίς; τί;	who? what?
τρέπομαι	turn, turn in flight
τυγχάνω	(+ nom. part.) happen to be –ing, be actually –ing

τύπτω	strike, hit	φέρω	carry, bear
ὕβρις -εως, ἡ	aggression, violence	φθάνω	anticipate X (acc.) in –ing (part.)
*ὑπηρέτης -ου, ὁ	servant, slave	φόβος -ου, ὁ	fear
φαίνομαι	appear to be, seem to be (+ part.)	ὦ	what ...! (+ gen.)

Vocabulary for Section 5

ἄδικος-ον	unjust
αἰτία -ας, ἡ	reason, cause, responsibility
αἴτιος-α-ον	(+ gen.) responsible (for), guilty (of)
†ἅπτω	light; fasten, fix
αὔριον	tomorrow
*βαθύς-εῖα-ύ	deep
*βαρύς-εῖα-ύ	heavy, weighty
βίος -ου, ὁ	life, means, livelihood
γάμος -ου, ὁ	marriage
†γε	at least (denotes some sort of reservation)
δέχομαι	receive
†διαλέγομαι	converse
†διανοέομαι	intend, plan
†διάνοια -ας, ἡ	intention, plan
διδάσκω	teach
δίκαιος-α-ον	just
δίκη -ης, ἡ	lawsuit, justice, penalty
*δίκην λαμβάνω	exact one's due, punish (παρά + gen.)
διότι	because
†δυστυχής-ές	unlucky
εἶμι	I shall go
εἰσέρχομαι	enter
εἰσφέρω	bring, carry in
ἔνδον	inside
†ἔνειμι	be in
*ἡδύς-εῖα-ύ	sweet, pleasant
ἵππος -ου, ὁ	horse
†καὶ δὴ καί	moreover
κακὰ ποιέω,	treat badly,
κακῶς ποιέω	do harm to
κολάζω	punish
κόπτω	knock (on), cut
λόγος -ου, ὁ	argument; word, speech; story, tale, reason
μαθητής -οῦ, ὁ	student
νεανίας -ου, ὁ	young man
νέος-α-ον	young
†νοῦς νοῦ, ὁ	mind, sense
*οἰκέτης -ου, ὁ	house-slave
ὅλος-η-ον	whole of
†οὐδέποτε	never
†οὐδέπω, οὔπω	not yet
οὔτε ... οὔτε	neither ... nor
*ὀφείλω	owe
πατήρ πατρός, ὁ	father
παύω	stop
πείθομαι	(+ dat.) believe, trust, obey
πείθω	persuade
*Ποσειδῶν -ῶνος, ὁ	Poseidon, god of the sea
πότε;	when?
πως	somehow
σοφιστής -οῦ, ὁ	sophist, thinker
σοφός-ή-όν	wise, clever
†σχεδόν	near, nearly; almost
τότε	then
υἱός -οῦ, ὁ	son
†φής	you (sing.) say
φιλέω	love, kiss
*χρέα -ων, τά	debts
χρήματα -ων, τά	money
†χρηστός-ή-όν	good, fine, serviceable

Vocabulary for Section 6

†ἄγροικος-ον	from the country, boorish
ἀδύνατος-ον	impossible
Ἀθῆναι -ῶν, αἱ	Athens
†ἀμαθής-ές	ignorant
ἀπέρχομαι	go away, depart
†ἄρα	then, in that case, consequently
*βάλλ' ἐς κόρακας	go to hell!
βιάζομαι	use force
γέρων -οντος, ὁ	old man
γνώμη -ης, ἡ	judgement, mind, purpose, plan
†δάκνω	bite, worry
*δεξιά -ᾶς, ἡ	right hand
*δεξιός-ά-όν	right, clever
δῆμος -ου, ὁ	people, deme
δῆτα	then
δράω	do, act
εἰ	if
†εἶτα	then, next
ἐκβάλλω	throw out
ἐμαυτόν -ήν	myself
ἐν νῷ ἔχω	intend, have in mind
ἐξευρίσκω	find out, discover
ἕτερος-α-ον	one (or the other) of two
†ἥλιος -ου, ὁ	sun
†ἥττων ἧττον	weaker, lesser
θαυμάζω	wonder at, be amazed at, admire
καίπερ	(+ part.) despite, although
κεφαλή -ῆς, ἡ	head
κλέπτω	steal
†κρείττων κρεῖττον	stronger, greater
λύω	release
†ὁπόσος-η-ον	how many, much
ὅπου	where? where
ὅτε	when
†οὐρανός -οῦ, ὁ	sky, heavens
*οὗτος	hey there! you there!
†ὀφρύς -ύος, ἡ	eyebrow
πάνυ	very (much); at all
*πηδάω	leap, jump
†πόρρω	far, afar off
†πότερος-α-ον	which (of two)?
πούς ποδός, ὁ	foot
πρῶτον	first, at first
πρῶτος-η-ον	first
ῥᾴδιος-α-ον	easy
ῥᾳδίως	easily
*σελήνη -ης, ἡ	moon
σός σή σόν	your(s) (sing.)
*Σωκράτης -ους, ὁ	Socrates
τήμερον	today
τί;	why?
*τίθημι	put, place
*φροντίς -ίδος, ἡ	thought, care, concern
†χρήσιμος-η-ον	useful, profitable
χωρίον -ου, τό	place, space, region
*ὡς	as

Vocabulary for Section 7

ἄγω	lead, bring
ἀλήθεια -ας, ἡ	truth
ἀνάγκη -ης, ἡ	necessity
ἀνάγκη ἐστί	(+ acc. or dat. and inf.) it is necessary (for X to do Y)
*ἀναιρέω	pick up
ἀνδρεῖος-α-ον	brave, manly
ἀποβαίνω	leave, depart
ἀποκρίνομαι	answer
ἀποφαίνω	reveal, show
ἀρετή -ῆς, ἡ	virtue, excellence
αὐτός-ή-ό	self
βούλομαι	wish, want
γὰρ δή	really, I assure you
γελάω	laugh
δεῖ	(+ acc. and inf.) it is necessary
δήπου	of course, surely
διαβαίνω	cross
*διαβάλλω	slander
*διαβολή -ῆς, ἡ	slander
διαφθείρω	corrupt, kill, destroy
διδάσκαλος -ου, ὁ	teacher
δοκέω	seem, consider oneself to be
δόξα -ης, ἡ	reputation, opinion
δύναμαι	be able
δύο	two
ἑαυτόν-ήν-ό	himself, herself, itself
εἰδώς εἰδυῖα εἰδός (part. of οἶδα)	knowing
εἶμι	I shall go
*ἐκδέχομαι	receive in turn
ἐμαυτόν-ήν	myself
*ἐμπίπτω	fall into, fall upon
ἐντεῦθεν	from then, from there
ἐξετάζω	question closely
ἐπαινέω	praise, agree
ἐπανέρχομαι	return
ἕπομαι	(+ dat.) follow
εὐθύς	at once, straightaway
εὑρίσκω	find, come upon
ἔφην (impf. of φημί)	I said
ἤ	than
*ἦ δ' ὅς	he said
*ᾖα (impf. of εἶμι)	I came from/went
ἥδομαι	(+ dat.) enjoy, be pleased with
*ἦν δ' ἐγώ	I said
ἰέναι (inf. of εἶμι)	to go
ἴσως	perhaps
*καταλαμβάνω	overtake, come across, seize
κτῆμα -ατος, τό	possession
λογίζομαι	reckon, calculate, consider
μάχη -ης, ἡ	fight, battle
μέντοι	however, but
μετά	(+ acc.) after
μή	no, not, don't
*νεανίσκος -ου, ὁ	young man
νοέω	think, mean, intend, notice
νομίζω	think, acknowledge
ὁ αὐτός	the same
οἰκέω	dwell in, live

οἶμαι	think
ὁμολογέω	agree
*οὔκουν	not ... therefore
*οὐκοῦν	therefore
πάλιν	back, again
πάρειμι	(+ dat.) be at hand, be present
πειράομαι	test, try
ποιητής -οῦ, ὁ	poet
πολλάκις	many times, often
ποταμός -οῦ, ὁ	river
ποτε	once, ever
*προτρέπω	urge on, impel
σ(ε)αυτόν-ήν	yourself (sing.)
σημεῖον -ου, τό	sign, signal
σοφία -ας, ἡ	wisdom
ὑμέτερος-α-ον	your (pl.)
φημί	I say
φιλοσοφία -ας, ἡ	philosophy
φυλάττω	guard
φωνέω	speak, utter
φωνή -ῆς, ἡ	voice, language, speech
ᾤμην (imperf. of οἶμαι)	I thought
ὡς	that

Vocabulary for Section 8

ἀγορά -ᾶς, ἡ	market-place, agora
ἄγω	live in, be at; lead, bring
ἀδικέω	be unjust, do wrong, commit a crime
*ᾄδω / ἀείδω	sing
ἀνίσταμαι	get up, stand up, emigrate
ἄξιος-α-ον	(+ gen.) worth, worthy of
ἀπολέω	I shall kill, destroy
βέλτιστος-η-ον	best
βελτίων-ον	better
*δεξιός-ά-όν	right, clever; right-hand
δῆμος -ου, ὁ	people, deme
διά	(+ gen.) through
*δικαστήριον -ου, τό	law-court
*δικαστής -οῦ, ὁ	juror, dikast
ἐγγύς	(+ gen.) near
*εἰρήνη -ης, ἡ	peace
*εἰρήνην ἄγω	live in peace, be at peace
ἐκεῖσε	(to) there
*ἐκκλησία -ας , ἡ	assembly, ekklesia
ἐν τούτῳ	meanwhile
ἐναντίον	(+ gen.) opposite, in front of
ἐπεί	since
ἐπί	(+ gen.) on
ἑτοῖμος-η-ον	ready to (+ inf.)
*εὐδαίμων-ον	happy, rich, blessed by the gods
ἡγεμών -όνος, ὁ	leader
ἡγέομαι	think, consider; lead (+ dat.)
ἡδονή -ῆς , ἡ	pleasure
*Ἡρακλῆς -έους, ὁ	Herakles
καθοράω	see, look down on
*κόραξ -ακος, ὁ	crow
λαμβάνομαι	(+ gen.) take hold of
μέγιστος-η-ον	greatest
μείζων-ον	greater
μετά	(+ gen.) with
μόνος-η-ον	alone
*μῶν;	surely not?
νυν	then (cf. νῦν = now)
ὁ μέν ... ὁ δέ	one ... another
οἰκτίρω	pity
*πάθος -ους, τό	suffering, experience
πανταχοῦ	everywhere
πέμπω	send
περί	(+ gen.) about
πλέως-α-ων	(+ gen.) full of
ποιέομαι	make
πολίτης -ου, ὁ	citizen
προστρέχω	run towards
*ῥήτωρ -ορος, ὁ	orator, politician
σῖτος -ου, ὁ	food
σπονδαί -ῶν, αἱ	treaty, truce
συγγενής -οῦς , ὁ	relation
*τᾶν	my dear chap (condescending)
ὑπέρ	(+ gen.) for, on behalf of
ὑπό	(+ gen.) by, at the hands of
φιλόσοφος -ου, ὁ	philosopher
χαῖρε	greetings! hello! farewell!
χαλεπός-ή-όν	difficult, hard
χείρ χειρός, ἡ	hand
χείρων-ον	worse
χρόνος -ου, ὁ	time

Vocabulary for Section 9

αἱρέω	take, capture, convict
αἰτέω	ask (for)
ἀμείνων-ον	better
ἀμφότεροι-αι-α	both
ἀναμένω	wait, hold on
ἄναξ -ακτος, ὁ	lord, prince, king
ἀναπείθω	persuade over to one's side
ἄνω	up, above
ἀπολογέομαι	defend oneself, make a speech in one's own defence
*ἀπολογία -ας, ἡ	defence speech
*ἀπολύω	acquit, release
ἀποτρέχω	run away
ἄρχομαι	begin to (+ inf. or part.), begin (+ gen.)
*ἀτάρ	but
αὖ	again, moreover
*βαρέως φέρω	take badly, find hard to bear
*γραφή -ῆς, ἡ	indictment, charge, case
*γραφὴν γράφομαι	indict on a charge (+ acc. of person and gen. of charge)
*γράφομαι	indict, charge
δεινός-ή-όν	terrible, dire, clever at (+ inf.)
*δικάζω	be a juror, make a judgement
διώκω	pursue, prosecute
δοκεῖ	it seems a good idea to X (dat.) to Y (inf.), X (dat.) decides to Y (inf.)
*δρᾶμα -ατος, τό	play, drama
ἐάω	allow
*ἐγκλείω	shut in, lock in
ἐθέλω	wish, want
ἐκτρέχω	run out
ἐκφέρω	carry out (e.g. for burial)
*ἐκφεύγω	escape
ἐλπίζω	hope, expect (+ fut. inf.)
ἕνεκα	(+ gen.) because, for the sake of (usually placed after the noun)
ἐνθάδε	here
ἐνταῦθα	here, at this point, there, at that point
ἐντυγχάνω	meet with (+ dat.)
ἐξάγω	lead/bring out
ἐξαπατάω	deceive, trick
ἐξέρχομαι	go out, come out
ἔξεστι	(+ dat. and inf.) it is possible
ἐπεί	when, since
ἐπί (+ dat.)	on, for the purpose of
ἐπίσταμαι	know how to (+ inf.), understand
ἐσθίω	eat
ἡμέρα -ας, ἡ	day
*ἡμίονος -ου, ὁ	mule
ἥσυχος-ον	quiet, peaceful
θάνατος -ου, ὁ	death
*θεατής -οῦ, ὁ	spectator, member of the audience
καθίζομαι	sit down
καθίζω	sit down
*καταδικάζω	condemn, convict (+ gen. of person, + acc. of charge)
*κατηγορέω	prosecute (+ gen. of person, + acc. of charge)

*κατηγορία -ας, ἡ	prosecution speech
κλέπτης -ου, ὁ	thief
κύων κυνός, ὁ	dog
*μάρτυς, μάρτυρος, ὁ	witness
μέλας-αινα-αν	black
μέλλω	be about to (+ fut. inf.); hesitate (+ pres. inf.); intend
μέρος -ους, τό	part, share
μηκέτι	no longer
μιαρός-ά-όν	foul, polluted
ὅ τι;	what?
ὅδε ἥδε τόδε	this
ὅμοιος-α-ον	(+ dat.) like, similar to
ὅμως	nevertheless, however
ὄνομα -ατος, τό	name
ὅτι	because
παιδίον -ου, τό	child, slave
παρά	(+ gen.) from; (+ dat.) with, near
παρέχω	give to, provide
πᾶς πᾶσα πᾶν	all, whole, every
πλήν	(+ gen.) except
πλησίον	nearby, (+ gen.) near
πολύ	much
πονηρός-ά-όν	wicked, wretched
*πράγματα παρέχω	cause trouble
πρός	(+ gen.) in the name of, under the protection of; (+ dat.) near, in addition to
πῦρ πυρός, τό	fire
πωλέω	sell
στένω	groan
*συγγνώμην ἔχω	(+ dat.) forgive, pardon
σύν	(+ dat.) with (the help of)
τάλας-αινα-αν	wretched, unhappy
τοιοῦτος τοιαύτη τοιοῦτο	of this kind, of such a kind
τυγχάνω	hit, chance on, happen on, be subject to (+ gen.), happen (to), be actually (+ part.)
ὑπισχνέομαι	(+ fut. inf.) promise
ὕστερον	later, further
ὕστερος-α-ον	later, last (of two)
*ὑφαιρέομαι	steal, take for oneself by stealth
*φέρε (imperat. sing.)	come!
φεύγω	flee, be a defendant, be on trial
χράομαι	(+ dat.) use, employ
χρή	(+ acc. and inf.) it is necessary
*ψῆφος -ου , ἡ	vote, voting pebble

Consolidated vocabulary list

A

ἀγαθός-ή-όν	good, noble
ἄγε (imperat. sing. ἄγω)	come!
†ἀγορά -ᾶς, ἡ	market-place, agora
†ἄγροικος-ον	from the country, boorish
†ἄγω	lead, bring; live in, be at
†ἀδικέω	be unjust, wrong, commit a crime
ἄδικος-ον	unjust
ἀδύνατος-ον	impossible
*ᾄδω / ἀείδω	sing
ἀεί	always
ἀείδω	*see* ᾄδω
Ἀθῆναι -ῶν, αἱ	Athens
Ἀθηναῖος -ου, ὁ	Athenian
†αἱρέω	take, capture, convict
†αἰτέω	ask (for)
αἰτία -ας, ἡ	reason, cause, responsibility
αἴτιος-α-ον	responsible (for), guilty (of) (+ gen.)
ἀκούω	hear, listen to (+ gen. of person/thing), (+ acc. of sound)
ἀκριβῶς	accurately, closely
ἀκρόπολις -εως, ἡ	Acropolis
†ἀλήθεια -ας, ἡ	truth
ἀληθῆ -ῶν, τά	(neut. pl. of ἀληθής = true) the truth
ἀλλά	but
ἀλλήλους-ας-α	each other, one another
ἄλλος-η-ο	other, the rest of
ἅμα	at the same time
†ἀμαθής-ές	ignorant
†ἀμείνων-ον	better
†ἀμφότεροι-αι-α	both
ἀναβαίνω	go up, come up
†ἀνάγκη -ης, ἡ	necessity
†ἀνάγκη ἐστί	it is necessary (+ acc. and inf.)
*ἀναιρέω	pick up
†ἀναμένω	wait, hold on
†ἄναξ, ἄνακτος, ὁ	lord, prince, king
†ἀναπείθω	persuade over to one's side
ἀναχωρέω	retreat
†ἀνδρεῖος-α-ον	brave, manly
ἀνήρ ἀνδρός, ὁ	man
ἄνθρωπος -ου, ὁ	man, fellow
†ἀνίσταμαι	get up, stand up, emigrate
ἀνομία -ας, ἡ	lawlessness
†ἄνω	up, above
†ἄξιος-α-ον	(+ gen.) worth, worthy of
ἀπάγω	lead, take away
ἀπέρχομαι	go away, depart
ἀπό	(+ gen.) from, away from
†ἀποβαίνω	leave, depart
ἀποθνῄσκω	die
†ἀποκρίνομαι	answer
ἀποκτείνω	kill
†ἀπολέω	I shall kill, destroy
†ἀπολογέομαι	defend oneself, make a speech in defence
*ἀπολογία -ας, ἡ	defence speech
*ἀπολύω	acquit, release
ἀπορέω	be at a loss, have no resources

ἀπορία -ας , ἡ	perplexity, lack of provisions
†ἀποτρέχω	run away, run off
†ἀποφαίνω	reveal, show
ἀποφεύγω	escape, run off
ἀποχωρέω	go away, depart
†ἅπτω	light, fasten, fix
†ἄρα	then, in that case, consequently
ἆρα;	? *indicates question*
†ἀρετή -ῆς, ἡ,	virtue, excellence
ἄριστος-η-ον	best, very good
†ἄρχομαι	begin to (+ inf. or part.), begin (+ gen.)
*ἀσέβεια -ας, ἡ	irreverence to the gods
ἄστυ -εως, τό	city
*ἀτάρ	but
*ἀτιμάζω	hold in dishonour, dishonour
†αὖ	again, moreover
αὖθις	again
αὔριον	tomorrow
αὐτόν-ήν-ό	him, her, it, (pl.) them
†αὐτος-ή-ό	self, the same
*ἀφέλκω	drag off
ἀφικνέομαι	arrive, come

B

βαθέως	deeply
*βαθύς-εῖα-ύ	deep
βαίνω	go, come, walk
*βάλλ' ἐς κόρακας	go to hell!
βάρβαρος -ου, ὁ	barbarian, foreigner
*βαρέως φέρω	take badly, find hard to bear
*βαρύς-εῖα-ύ	heavy, weighty
βασιλεύς -έως, ὁ	king
βέβαιος-α-ον	secure
†βέλτιστος-η-ον	best
†βελτίων-ον	better
βιάζομαι	use force
βίος -ου, ὁ	life, means, livelihood
βλέπω	look (at)
βοάω	shout (for)
βοή -ῆς, ἡ	shout
βοηθέω	(+ dat.) run to help, help
†βούλομαι	wish, want
βραδέως	slowly
*βωμός -οῦ, ὁ	altar

Γ

γάμος -ου, ὁ	marriage
γάρ	for
†γὰρ δή	really, I assure you
†γε	at least (denotes some sort of reservation)
*γείτων -ονος, ὁ	neighbour
†γελάω	laugh
γέρων -οντος, ὁ	old man
γεωργός -οῦ, ὁ	farmer
γῆ, γῆς, ἡ	land, earth
γίγνομαι	become, be born, happen, arise
γιγνώσκω	know, think, resolve
γνώμη -ης, ἡ	judgement, mind, purpose, plan
*γραφή -ῆς, ἡ	indictment, charge, case
*γραφὴν γράφομαι	indict on a charge (+ acc. of person and gen. of charge)

*γράφομαι	indict, charge
γυνή γυναικός, ἡ	woman

Δ

*δαίμων -ονος, ὁ	god, daimon
†δάκνω	bite, worry
δέ	and, but
†δεῖ	it is necessary (+ acc. and inf.)
δεινός-ή-όν	terrible, dire, clever
†δεινός-ή-όν	clever (at) (+ inf.)
*δεξιά -ᾶς, ἡ	right hand
*δεξιός-ά-όν	right, clever; right-hand
δεσπότης -ου, ὁ	master
δεῦρο	here, over here
δέχομαι	receive
δή	then, indeed
δῆλος-η-ον	clear, obvious
δηλόω	show, reveal
δῆμος -ου, ὁ	people, deme
†δήπου	of course, surely
δῆτα	then
διά	(+ acc.) because of
†διά	(+ gen.) through
διὰ τί;	why?
†διαβαίνω	cross
*διαβάλλω	slander
*διαβολή -ῆς, ἡ	slander
†διαλέγομαι	converse
†διανοέομαι	intend, plan
†διάνοια -ας, ἡ	intention, plan
διαφθείρω	corrupt, destroy, kill
†διδάσκαλος -ου, ὁ	teacher
διδάσκω	teach
διέρχομαι	go through, relate
*δικάζω	be a juror, make a judgement
δίκαιος-α-ον	just
*δικαστήριον -ου, τό	law-court
*δικαστής -οῦ, ὁ	juror, dikast
δίκη -ης, ἡ	lawsuit, justice, penalty
*δίκην λαμβάνω	punish, exact one's due from (παρά + gen.)
διότι	because
†διώκω	pursue, prosecute
†δοκεῖ	it seems a good idea to X (dat.) to do Y (inf.), X (dat.) decides to Y (inf.)
†δοκέω	seem, consider oneself to be
†δόξα -ης, ἡ	reputation, opinion
δουλό-ομαι	enslave (for oneself)
δοῦλος -ου, ὁ	slave
*δρᾶμα -ατος, τό	play, drama
δράω	do, act
†δύναμαι	be able
†δύο	two
δύω	sink
†δυστυχής-ές	unlucky

E

†ἑαυτόν-ήν-ό	himself/herself/itself
†ἐάω	allow
ἐγγύς	(+ gen.) near, nearby
*ἐγκλείω	shut in, lock in
ἐγώ	I
ἔγωγε	I at least, for my part
†ἐθέλω	wish, want

εἰ	if
†εἰδώς εἰδυῖα εἰδός (part. of οἶδα)	knowing
εἰμί	be (I am etc.)
εἶμι	I shall go
εἰπέ (imperat. sing.)	speak! tell me!
*εἰρήνη -ης, ἡ	peace
*εἰρήνην ἄγω	live in peace, be at peace
εἰς	(+ acc.) to, into, onto
εἰσβαίνω	enter, board, go onto
εἰσέρχομαι	enter
εἰσφέρω	bring, carry in
†εἶτα	then, next
ἐκ, ἐξ	(+ gen.) out of
ἐκβάλλω	throw out
*ἐκδέχομαι	receive in turn
ἐκεῖνος-η-ο	that, s(he), it
†ἐκεῖσε	(to) there
*ἐκκλησία -ας, ἡ	assembly, ekklesia
†ἐκτρέχω	run out
†ἐκφέρω	carry out (e.g. for burial)
*ἐκφεύγω	escape
ἐλευθερία -ας, ἡ	freedom
ἐλεύθερος-α-ον	free
ἐλευθερόω	set free
*ἐλθέ (imperat. sing.)	come!
Ἕλλην -ηνος, ὁ	Greek
†ἐλπίζω	hope, expect (+ fut. inf.)
†ἐμαυτόν-ήν	myself
ἐμβαίνω	embark
ἐμός-ή-όν	my, mine
ἔμπειρος-ον	skilled, experienced
*ἐμπίπτω	fall into, fall upon
ἐμπόριον -ου, τό	market-place
ἐν	(+ dat.) in, on, among
ἐν νῷ ἔχω	intend, have in mind
†ἐν τούτῳ	meanwhile
†ἐναντίον	(+ gen.) opposite, in front of
ἔνδον	inside
†ἔνειμι	be in
†ἕνεκα	(+ gen.) because, for the sake of (usually placed after the noun)
†ἐνθάδε	here
†ἐνταῦθα	here, at this point, there, at that point
†ἐντεῦθεν	from then, from there
†ἐντυγχάνω	(+ dat.) meet with, come upon
†ἐξάγω	lead, bring out
†ἐξαπατάω	deceive, trick
†ἐξέρχομαι	go out, come out
†ἔξεστι	it is possible for X (dat.) to – (inf.)
†ἐξετάζω	question closely
ἐξευρίσκω	find out, discover
†ἐπαινέω	praise, agree
†ἐπανέρχομαι	return
†ἐπεί	when, since
ἐπειδή	when, since, because
ἔπειτα	then, next
ἐπέρχομαι	go against, attack
ἐπί	(+ acc.) at, against, to, to get
†ἐπί	(+ gen.) on; (+ dat.) on, for the purpose of
*ἐπικαλέομαι	call upon (to witness)
†ἐπίσταμαι	know how to (+ inf.), understand

†ἕπομαι	(+ dat.) follow
ἔργον -ου, τό	task, work, job, duty
ἔρχομαι	go, come
ἐρωτάω	ask
†ἐσθίω	eat
ἕτερος-α-ον	one (or the other) of two
ἔτι	still, yet
ἔτι καὶ νῦν	even now, still now
†ἑτοῖμος-η-ον	ready to (+ inf.)
εὖ	well
*εὐδαίμων-ον	happy, rich, blessed by the gods
†εὐθύς	at once, straightaway
†εὑρίσκω	find, come upon
εὔφρων εὖφρον	well-disposed
εὐχή -ῆς, ἡ	prayer
εὔχομαι	pray
†ἔφην (impf. of φημί)	I said
ἔχω	have, hold

Z

Ζεύς Διός, ὁ	Zeus
ζητέω	look for, seek

H

ἤ	or
†ἤ	than
*ἦ δ' ὅς	he said
*ᾖα (impf. εἶμι)	I came/went
†ἡγεμών -όνος, ὁ	leader
†ἡγέομαι	think, consider; lead (+ dat.)
ἡδέως	with pleasure, sweetly, happily
ἤδη	by now, now, already
†ἥδομαι	(+ dat.) enjoy, be pleased with
†ἡδονή -ῆς, ἡ	pleasure
*ἡδύς-εῖα-ύ	sweet, pleasant
†ἥλιος -ου, ὁ	sun
ἡμεῖς	we
†ἡμέρα -ας, ἡ	day
ἡμέτερος-α-ον	our(s)
*ἡμίονος -ου, ὁ	mule
*ἦν δ' ἐγώ	I said
*Ἡρακλῆς -έους, ὁ	Herakles
ἡσυχάζω	be quiet, keep quiet
ἡσυχία -ας, ἡ	quiet, peace
†ἥσυχος-ον	quiet, peaceful
†ἥττων ἧττον	lesser, weaker

Θ

θάλαττα -ης, ἡ	sea
†θάνατος -ου, ὁ	death
θαυμάζω	wonder at, be amazed at, admire
θεά -ᾶς, ἡ	goddess
θεάομαι	observe, watch, gaze at
*θεατής -οῦ, ὁ	spectator, member of the audience
θεός -οῦ, ὁ, ἡ	god(-dess)
θνητός-ή-όν	mortal
θόρυβος -ου, ὁ	noise, din
θύρα -ας, ἡ	door
θυσία -ας, ἡ	sacrifice
θύω	sacrifice

Ι

ἰδού (imperat. sing.)	look! here! hey!
†ἰέναι (inf. of εἶμι)	to go
ἱερόν -οῦ, τό	sanctuary
*ἱκέτης -ου, ὁ	suppliant
ἵππος -ου, ὁ	horse
†ἴσως	perhaps

Κ

καθεύδω	sleep
†καθίζομαι	sit down
†καθίζω	sit down
†καθοράω	see, look down on
καί	and, also, even
†καὶ δὴ καί	moreover
καίπερ	(+ part.) although, despite
*κακοδαίμων-ον	unlucky, dogged by an evil daimon
κακός-ή-όν	bad, evil, mean, cowardly, lowly
κακὰ ποιέω, κακῶς ποιέω	treat badly, do harm to
κακῶς	badly, evilly
καλέω	call, summon
κάλλιστος-η-ον	very fine, very good, most beautiful
καλός-ή-όν	fine, beautiful, good
καλῶς	well, finely, beautifully
κατά	(+ acc.) in, on, by, according to
καταβαίνω	go down, come down
*καταδικάζω	condemn, convict (+ gen. of person and acc. of charge)
*καταλαμβάνω	overtake, come across, seize
*κατηγορέω	prosecute (+ gen. of person and acc. of charge)
*κατηγορία -ας, ἡ	prosecution speech
*κελευστής -οῦ, ὁ	boatswain
κελεύω	order
κεφαλή -ῆς, ἡ	head
κῆρυξ -υκος, ὁ	herald
κίνδυνος -ου, ὁ	danger
†κλέπτης -ου, ὁ	thief
κλέπτω	steal
κολάζω	punish
κόπτω	knock (on), cut
*κόραξ -ακος, ὁ	crow
κρατέω	(+ gen.) hold sway/power over
†κρείττων-ον	stronger, greater
†κτῆμα -ατος, τό	possession
κυβερνήτης -ου, ὁ	captain, helmsman
†κύων κυνός, ὁ	dog
κωλύω	prevent, stop

Λ

Λακεδαιμόνιος -ου, ὁ	Spartan
†λαμβάνομαι	(+ gen.) take hold of
λαμβάνω	take, capture
*λαμπάς -άδος, ἡ	torch
λανθάνω	escape notice of X (acc.) in –ing (part.)
λέγω	speak, say, tell, mean
*λέμβος -ου, ὁ	boat, life-boat
λιμήν -ένος, ὁ	harbour
†λογίζομαι	calculate, reckon, consider
λόγος -ου, ὁ	story, tale, speech, word, reason, argument
λύω	release

M

*μά	(+ acc.) no, by ...! (e.g. μὰ Δία, no, by Zeus!)
μαθητής -οῦ, ὁ	student
μάλιστα	especially, particularly; yes
μανθάνω	learn, understand
*μάρτυς -υρος, ὁ	witness
†μάχη -ης, ἡ	fight, battle
μάχομαι	fight
μέγας μεγάλη μέγα	great, big
†μέγιστος-η-ον	greatest
†μείζων-ον	greater
†μέλας-αινα-αν	black
†μέλλω	be about to (+ fut. inf.); hesitate (+ pres. inf.); intend
μέν ... δέ	on the one hand ... on the other hand
†μέντοι	however, but
μένω	remain, wait for
†μέρος -ους, τό	part, share
†μετά	(+ acc.) after; (+ gen.) with
μή	no, not, don't
†μηκέτι	no longer
†μιαρός-ά-όν	foul, polluted
μισέω	hate
†μόνος-η-ον	alone
*μῶν;	surely not?
μῶρος-α-ον	stupid, foolish

N

ναί	yes
ναυμαχία -ας, ἡ	naval battle
ναῦς νεώς, ἡ	ship
ναύτης -ου, ὁ	sailor
ναυτικός-ή-όν	naval
νεανίας -ου, ὁ	young man
*νεανίσκος -ου, ὁ	young man
νεκρός -οῦ, ὁ	corpse
νέος-α-ον	young
*νεώριον -ου, τό	dockyard
*νή	(+ acc.) yes, by ...! (e.g. νὴ Δία, yes, by Zeus!)
νῆσος -ου, ἡ	island
νικάω	conquer, win, defeat
νίκη -ης, ἡ	victory, conquest
†νοέω	think, mean, intend, notice
†νομίζω	acknowledge, think
νόμος -ου, ὁ	law, convention
νόσος -ου, ἡ	illness, plague, disease
†νοῦς νοῦ, ὁ	mind, sense
†νυν	then
νῦν	now
νύξ, νυκτός, ἡ	night

Ξ

ξεῖνος / ξένος -ου, ὁ	foreigner, guest, host

O

ὁ ἡ τό	the
†ὁ αὐτός	the same
†ὁ μέν ... ὁ δέ	one ... another
†ὅ τι;	what?
†ὅδε, ἥδε, τόδε	this
οἷ	(to) where
οἶδα	know

οἴκαδε	homewards
*οἰκέτης -ου, ὁ	house-slave
†οἰκέω	dwell in, live
οἴκησις -εως, ἡ	dwelling
οἰκία -ας, ἡ	house
οἴκοι	at home
†οἰκτίρω	pity
†οἶμαι	think
*οἴμοι	alas! oh dear!
ὀλίγος -η -ον	small, few
ὅλος-η-ον	whole of
*ὀλοφύρομαι	lament, mourn for
†ὅμοιος-α-ον	(+ dat.) like, similar to
†ὁμολογέω	agree
*ὁμόνοια -ας, ἡ	agreement, harmony
†ὅμως	nevertheless, however
†ὄνομα -ατος, τό	name
ὅπλα -ων, τά	weapons, arms
†ὁπόσος-η-ον	how many, much
†ὁπότε	when
ὅπου	where?, where
ὁράω	see
ὀρθός-ή-όν	straight, correct, right
ὅσος-η-ον	how great
ὅτε	when
ὅτι	that
†ὅτι	because
οὐ, οὐκ, οὐχ	no, not
οὐδέ	and not, not even
οὐδείς, οὐδεμία, οὐδέν	no, no one, nothing
†οὐδέποτε	never
†οὐδέπω	not yet
οὐκέτι	no longer
*οὐκοῦν	therefore
*οὔκουν	not ... therefore
οὖν	so, then, really, therefore
οὔπω	not yet
†οὐρανός -οῦ, ὁ	sky, heavens
οὔτε ... οὔτε	neither ... nor
*οὗτος	hey there! you there!
οὗτος αὕτη τοῦτο	this, (s)he, it
οὑτοσί αὑτηί τουτί	this here
οὕτω/οὕτως	thus, so, in this way
*ὀφείλω	owe
†ὀφρύς -ύος, ἡ	eyebrow

Π

*πάθος -ους, τό	suffering, experience
†παιδίον -ου, τό	child, slave
παίζω (πρός + acc.)	play, joke at
παῖς παιδός, ὁ	child, slave
†πάλιν	back, again
†πανταχοῦ	everywhere
πάνυ	very (much); at all
παρά	(+ acc.) along, beside
†παρά	(+ gen.) from; (+ dat.) with, near
†πάρειμι	(+ dat.), be at hand, be present
†παρέχω	give to, provide
Παρθενών -ῶνος ὁ	the Parthenon
†πᾶς πᾶσα πᾶν	all, whole, every
πάσχω	suffer, experience, undergo
πατήρ πατρός, ὁ	father

πατρίς -ίδος, ἡ	fatherland
παύομαι	stop, cease (+ part.)
παύω	stop
πείθομαι	(+ dat.) believe, trust, obey
πείθω	persuade
†πειράομαι	test, try
†πέμπω	send
περί	(+ acc.) about, concerning
†περί	(+ gen.) about
*πηδάω	leap, jump
πίπτω	fall, die
πλέω	sail
†πλέως-α-ων	(+ gen.) full of
πλῆθος -ους, τό	number, crowd, the people
†πλήν	(+ gen.) except
†πλησίον	nearby, (+ gen.) near
πλοῖον-ου, τό	vessel, ship
πόθεν;	from where?
ποῖ;	where to?
†ποιέομαι	make
ποιέω	make, do
†ποιητής -οῦ, ὁ	poet
πολέμιοι -ῶν, οἱ	the enemy
πολέμιος-α-ον	hostile, enemy
πόλεμος -ου, ὁ	war
πόλις -εως, ἡ	city, city-state
†πολίτης -ου, ὁ	citizen
πολλά (neut. pl. of πολύς)	many things
†πολλάκις	many times, often
†πολύ	much
πολύς πολλή πολύ	much, many
†πονηρός-ά-όν	wicked, wretched
πορεύομαι	march, journey, go
†πόρρω	far, afar off
*Ποσειδῶν -ῶνος, ὁ	Poseidon, god of the sea
†ποταμός -οῦ, ὁ	river
†ποτε	once, ever
πότε;	when?
πότερον ... ἤ	whether ... or
†πότερος-α-ον	which (of two)?
που	somewhere, anywhere
ποῦ;	where?
πούς, ποδός, ὁ	foot
πρᾶγμα -ατος, τό	thing, matter, affair, (pl.) troubles
*πράγματα παρέχω	cause trouble
πρέσβεις -εων, οἱ	ambassadors
*πρεσβευτής -οῦ, ὁ	ambassador
πρός	(+ acc.) to, towards
†πρός	(+ gen.) in the name of, under the protection of
†πρός	(+ dat.) in addition to, near
προσέρχομαι	go/come towards, advance
†προστρέχω	run towards
*προτρέπω	urge on, impel
πρῶτον	first, at first
πρῶτος-η-ον	first
†πῦρ, πυρός, τό	fire
*πυρά -ᾶς, ἡ	funeral pyre
*πυρά -ῶν, τά	fire-signal
†πωλέω	sell
πῶς;	how?
πως	somehow
πῶς γὰρ οὔ;	of course

Ρ

ῥᾴδιος-α-ον	easy
ῥᾳδίως	easily
*ῥαψῳδός-οῦ, ὁ	rhapsode
*ῥήτωρ -ορος, ὁ	orator, politician
ῥίπτω	throw

Σ

σαφῶς	clearly
σ(ε)αυτόν-ήν	yourself (sing.)
*σελήνη -ης, ἡ	moon
†σημεῖον -ου, τό	sign, signal
†σῖτος -ου, ὁ	food
σιωπάω	be silent
*σκεύη -ων, τά	gear, furniture
σκοπέω	look at, consider, examine
σός σή σόν	your (sing.)
†σοφία -ας, ἡ	wisdom
σοφιστής -οῦ, ὁ	sophist, thinker
σοφός-ή-όν	wise, clever
*σπένδω	pour a libation
σπεύδω	hurry
†σπονδαί -ῶν, αἱ	treaty, truce
*σπονδή -ῆς, ἡ	libation
†στένω	groan
στρατηγός -οῦ, ὁ	general
στρατιά -ᾶς, ἡ	army
σύ	you (sing.)
†συγγενής -οῦς, ὁ	relation
*συγγνώμην ἔχω	(+ dat.) forgive, pardon
†σύν	(+ dat.) with (the help of)
†σχεδόν	near, nearly, almost
σῴζω	save, keep safe
*Σωκράτης -ους, ὁ	Socrates
σῶος-α-ον	safe
σωτήρ -ῆρος, ὁ	saviour
σωτηρία -ας, ἡ	safety

Τ

*τὰ ναυτικά	lit. 'the naval-things', naval matters
*τὰ στρατηγικά	lit. 'the leader's-things', leadership, generalship
*τὰ στρατιωτικά	lit. 'the soldier's-things', military matters
†τάλας-αινα-αν	wretched, unhappy
*τᾶν	my dear chap (condescending)
*τάξις -εως, ἡ	order, rank, battle-array
ταχέως	quickly
τε ... καί	both ... and
τέλος	in the end, finally
τέχνη -ης, ἡ	skill, art, expertise
τήμερον	today
τι	a, something
τί;	what? why?
*τίθημι	put, place
τιμάω	honour
τις, τι	a, a certain (man, etc.), someone (thing)
τίς; τί;	who? what? which?
†τοιοῦτος τοιαύτη τοιοῦτο	of this kind, of such a kind
τόλμα -ης, ἡ	daring
τολμάω	dare, be daring, undertake
τότε	then
τρέπομαι	turn (self), turn in flight

τρέχω	run
*τριήραρχος -ου, ὁ	trierarch
τυγχάνω (+ nom. part.)	happen to be –ing, be actually –ing
†τυγχάνω	hit, chance on, happen on, be subject to (+ gen.)
τύπτω	strike, hit

Υ

ὕβρις -εως, ἡ	aggression, violence, insult, humiliation
υἱός -οῦ, ὁ	son
ὑμεῖς	you (pl.)
†ὑμέτερος-α-ον	your (pl.)
†ὑπέρ	(+ gen.) for, on behalf of
*ὑπηρέτης -ου, ὁ	servant, slave
†ὑπισχνέομαι	(+ fut. inf.) promise
†ὑπό	(+ gen.) by, at the hands of
†ὕστερον	later, further
†ὕστερος-α-ον	later, last (of two)
*ὑφαιρέομαι	steal, take for oneself by stealth

Φ

φαίνομαι	appear to be, seem to be (+ part.)
*φέρε (imperat. sing.)	come!
φέρω	carry, bear
φεύγω	run off, flee
†φεύγω	be a defendant, be on trial
†φημί	I say
†φής	you (sing.) say
φθάνω	anticipate X (acc.) in –ing (part.)
φιλέω	love, kiss
φίλος -ου, ὁ	friend
φίλος-η-ον	dear, friendly, one's own
†φιλοσοφία -ας, ἡ	philosophy
†φιλόσοφος -ου, ὁ	philosopher
φοβέομαι	fear, be afraid of, respect
φόβος -ου, ὁ	fear
φροντίζω	think, worry
*φροντίς -ίδος, ἡ	thought, care, concern
†φυλάττω	guard
†φωνέω	speak, utter
†φωνή -ῆς, ἡ	voice, language, speech

Χ

†χαῖρε	greetings! hello! farewell!
†χαλεπός-ή-όν	difficult, hard
†χείρ χειρός, ἡ	hand
†χείρων χεῖρον	worse
†χράομαι	(+ dat.) use, employ
*χρέα -ῶν, τά	debts
†χρή	it is necessary for X (acc.) to – (inf.)
χρήματα -ων, τά	money
†χρήσιμος-η-ον	profitable, useful
†χρηστός-ή-όν	good, fine, serviceable
†χρόνος -ου, ὁ	time
χωρέω	go, come
χωρίον -ου, τό	place, space, region

Ψ

ψευδῶς	falsely
*ψῆφος -ου, ἡ	vote, voting pebble

Ω

ὦ	what ...! (+ gen.)
ὦ	O (when addressing someone, as in 'O Socrates')
†ᾤμην (imperf. of οἶμαι)	I thought
ὡς	how!
†ὡς	that
*ὡς	as
ὥσπερ	like, as

Glossary

accent There are three accents in Greek: the acute (´), the grave (`) and the circumflex (˜). These markings are placed on vowels to indicate the tone or musical pitch at which syllables were pronounced by ancient speakers. In this module you are not required to mimic the rising and falling pitch of ancient Greek in pronunciation – neither will you be asked to write accents, except in the case of a very small number of words where accentuation affects meaning, e.g. τίς, *who*?, cf. τις, *a*, *a certain*.

accusative The case of the direct object of the verb, e.g. τὸν στρατηγὸν ὁρᾷ ὁ ναύτης, the sailor sees *the general.* For information on the accusative case, see Section 3 'Cases and their uses'.

active In Greek, the dictionary form of most active verbs ends in -ω, e.g. παύω, ποιέω, ὁράω, etc. 'Active' is one of the three voices in Greek, the others being middle and passive. (For information about the difference between the active and middle forms of verbs, see Appendix Four.)

adjective A 'describing word': that is to say, a word that modifies (i.e. describes) a noun, e.g. *beautiful, brave, large.* In vocabulary lists, adjectives are given with their masculine/feminine/neuter endings, e.g. καλός-ή-όν, *beautiful*, etc. Adjectives must agree in number, gender and case with the noun they describe (see agreement).

adverb A word which modifies (describes the action of) a verb, e.g. *quickly, fast, well, never.* Adverbs can also modify an adjective or another adverb: *particularly nice*; *really quickly.* Most adverbs in Greek end in -ως, e.g. κακῶς, *badly*; σαφῶς, *clearly.*

agreement In the case of verbs, agreement means the change in the form of the verb depending on the verb's subject. Thus in the sentence 'I do', *do* **agrees** with *I*; in the sentence 'he does', *does* **agrees** with *he*. In the case of adjectives (and the definite article), agreement means the change in the form of the adjective to match the number, gender and case of the noun: thus ὁ καλὸς θεός, *the beautiful god*, but ἡ καλὴ θεά, *the beautiful goddess*.

aorist Verbs in the aorist describe complete actions, e.g. ἔπαυσα, *I stopped*; ἦλθον, *I went.* In the case of verb-forms like these, which carry an augment (i.e. finite verbs), the aorist generally indicates that the event being described is seen as a single completed action in the past. In the case of infinitives, imperatives and participles, however, the difference between present and aorist forms of the verb is one not of time but of aspect.

aspect The name for the different ways that Greek has of conceiving of the nature of an action, e.g. as imperfective (ongoing process) or aorist (as a complete event). See *G&E*, pp. 144–5, §165.

augment The modification of the beginning of the stem of finite verbs when they appear in the imperfect and aorist tense, e.g. ἔπαυον, *I was stopping*; ἔπαυσα, *I stopped.* Most commonly the letter ἐ- is added (as in ἔπαυσα, etc.): the technical name for this is a 'syllabic augment'. When the verb stem begins with a vowel, however, this vowel lengthens if it can; e.g. ἀκούω becomes ἤκουσα in the aorist (i.e. ἀ lengthens to ἠ): the technical name for this is a 'temporal augment'. For information on augments, see Appendix One.

breathing The marks (ʽ) and (ʼ) which appear at the beginning of words that start with a vowel (α, ε, η, ι, ο, υ, ω) or rho (ϱ). The rough breathing indicates that the word began with a(n) 'h' sound, e.g. ὁϱάω, *I see*; ὡς, *how*; whereas the smooth breathing indicates that there was no 'h' sound, e.g. ἐκ, *out of*; οὐδέν, *nothing.*

case Greek nouns are found in one of five cases: nominative, accusative, genitive, dative and vocative. See Section 3 'Cases and their uses'.

clause A section of a sentence containing, as a minimum, a subject and a verb. See Section 4 'Sentence structure'.

comparative In English, the form of the adjective that gives it the meaning 'more', or '–er': e.g. *more beautiful, bigger, better.* In Greek, a comparative adjective can be translated in a number of ways: e.g. σοφώτεϱος can be translated not only as 'wiser' but also 'rather wise', 'fairly wise' or 'quite wise', according to context.

(subject) complement A word or phrase which adds to the description of the subject of a sentence (and which therefore, like the subject, appears in the nominative case). A (subject) complement is most often found in conjunction with a 'linking verb' like εἰμί, *be*, or γίγνομαι, *become.* Thus ὁ ναύτης γίγνεται φιλόσοφος, *the sailor becomes a philosopher*, where φιλόσοφος, *philosopher*, is the complement of the subject, ναύτης, *sailor.*

compound verb A verb formed by adding a prefix (usually a preposition in Greek) to a simple verb: e.g. ἀπο-φεύγω, *escape, run off*; εἰσ-έϱχομαι, *enter, go in.*

conjunction A word that links parts of a sentence, e.g. *and, since, because.*

conjugation The way in which verbs change according to number and person, e.g. παύω, παύεις, παύει, etc. Verbs are conjugated, nouns (and adjectives) are declined.

contract verb A verb whose stem ends in α, ε, or ο; e.g. ὁϱάω, *I see*; ποιέω, *I do/make*; δουλόομαι, *I enslave.* These vowels (α, ε, and ο) 'contract' with the verb endings: e.g. ὁϱά-ω contracts to ὁϱῶ, *I see*; ὁϱά-ει contracts to ὁϱᾷ, *he/she/it sees*. It is these contracted forms that appear in the reading passages in *Reading Greek.*

crasis Crasis occurs when the vowel or diphthong at the end of a word coalesces with one at the beginning of the next word, e.g. ὦνδρες instead of ὦ ἄνδρες.

dative The 'to' or 'for' case: as in the sentences παρέχω τὰ χρήματα τῷ Ἡγεστράτῳ, *I give the money to Hegestratos*; οἱ παῖδες τὰ χρήματα τῷ πατρὶ ἔκλεψαν, *the children stole the money for their father.* For information on the dative case, see Section 3 'Cases and their uses'.

declension The different ways in which nouns change according to their number and case, e.g. ἄνθρωπος (nom.), ἄνθρωπον (acc.), etc. Similarly the name given to how the definite article and adjectives change according to number, gender and case. Nouns (and adjectives) are declined, verbs are conjugated.

definite article In English, 'the'. In Greek, the definite article changes according to the noun with which it agrees, e.g. ὁ ἄνθρωπος, *the man* (masculine singular nominative) but τὰ πλοῖα, *the ships* (neuter plural nominative/accusative). See *G&E*, pp. 8–9, §8.

diphthong A combination of two vowels pronounced as one sound, e.g. αι, ει, οι.

(direct) object The person or thing in a sentence that 'suffers' or 'experiences' the action of the verb. In the sentence 'The man strikes the door', for example, 'the man' is the subject, 'strikes' the verb and 'the door' is the direct object (i.e. it is the door that 'experiences' the striking). In Greek, the direct object of a verb appears in the accusative case.

direct speech The actual words delivered by a speaker.

elision The loss of a vowel from the end of one word when the next word begins with a vowel, e.g. δεῦρ᾽ ἐλθέ, *come here*! (instead of δεῦρο ἐλθέ).

enclitic A word which is accentually linked to the previous word, often resulting in a change in that word's accentuation (the word 'enclitic' derives from the Greek ἐγκλίνω, *lean on*). Common examples include τε, *and*, and τις, τι, *a certain*: thus ἄνθρωπος, but ἄνθρωπός τις (with an acute accent on the last syllable of ἄνθρωπος). See *G&E*, p. 377, §347.

ending The letters added to the stem of a noun, verb or adjective, for example, in order to mark case, number, gender, and so on. Thus the ending of παύεις, *you* (s.) *stop* – -εις – indicates that the verb is second person singular.

feminine One of the three genders of Greek nouns. In vocabulary lists, feminine nouns are distinguished by the definite article ἡ: e.g. ἡ νίκη, *victory.*

finite verb A verb with a personal ending, like παύομεν, *we stop* or ἔρχονται, *they come/go*; i.e. one whose ending indicates the number and person of its subject (-ομεν = *we*; -ονται = *they*). Infinitives and participles are ***not*** finite verbs.

gender Nouns and adjectives are one of three genders: masculine, feminine or neuter. Like adjectives, the definite article, participles and some pronouns change according to gender, too: e.g. ὁ θεός, *the god*; but ἡ θεά (or even ἡ θεός), *the goddess*.

genitive The 'of' case: e.g. τὸ τοῦ Ἡγεστράτου πλοῖον, *the ship of Hegestratos* (or *Hegestratos' ship*). For information about the genitive case, see Section 3 'Cases and their uses'.

imperative The form of the verb used to issue a command, e.g. παῦε, *stop*!, πείθου, *obey*!

imperfect tense The tense used to describe ongoing or incomplete actions in the past, e.g. ἔλεγον, *I was speaking*, *I used to speak* (or *I spoke* when the 'speaking' went on regularly in the past: 'I spoke to my mother every day').

impersonal verb In English, a verb occurring in the 'it'-form, when 'it' does not refer to anything specific, e.g. 'it is raining', 'it seems', 'it is (necessary)', etc.

indefinite article In English the indefinite article is *a* or *an*. The nearest equivalent word in Greek is τις, τι, *a* (*certain*), e.g. ἄνθρωπός τις, *a certain man*. (Note that the plural of τις, τι – τινές, τινά – may be translated 'some'.)

indicative The mood in Greek most commonly used to make statements (and to ask simple questions). The indicative is the mood of most of the verbs met in this module (the other moods in Greek being the imperative, optative and subjunctive). Stating that a verb is in the indicative also signifies that it is not in an infinitive or participle, but rather a finite verb.

indirect object Used most frequently with verbs of giving or saying, the indirect object in English is the person (or thing) ***to whom*** something is said or given (or less often, ***for whom*** something is done). In Greek, the indirect object is expressed by the dative: e.g. λέγω τοῖς ἀνθρώποις, *I speak to the men*; παρέχω τὰ χρήματα τῇ γυναικί, *I give the money to the woman*; τοὺς ἵππους τῷ πατρὶ ἔκλεψα, *I stole the horses for my father.*

indirect question The reporting of an actual, direct question. In the sentence 'The woman asked me when I had arrived' the underlined section is an indirect question; the original question that the woman asked being 'When did you arrive?'

indirect statement The reporting of someone's words, e.g. 'The sailor said that the general was coming tonight' (the original statement that the sailor made being 'The general is coming tonight'). On ways of forming indirect statements in Greek, see Section 4 'Sentence structure'.

infinitive	Examples of infinitives in English include *to be, to go, to have, to stop*. In Greek, regular present infinitives generally end in either -ειν or -εσθαι, e.g. παύειν, *to stop*; ἔρχεσθαι, *to come/go*. (Infinitives also exist in other tenses apart from the present, both in English and in Greek.)
inflection	The way in which words change shape to convey information about their precise meaning and/or their grammatical role in a sentence (e.g. English 'he'/'him', 'is'/'are', 'desk'/'desks', 'look'/'looked'). Languages like Greek that rely heavily on inflection to convey meaning are often called 'inflected languages'.
interjection	A word or phrase that is not connected grammatically to the rest of the sentence and which is used to convey emotion, e.g. *hey*! *oh dear*! *alas*! *whoops*! *wow*!
intransitive verb	A verb that does ***not*** take a direct object. Some verbs are intransitive by nature, e.g. *die*, *talk*, whereas other verbs can be used both transitively and intransitively, e.g. open: 'she opened the show that evening' (where 'show' is the direct object – transitive use); 'the doors opened at six' (where there is no direct object – intransitive use).
iota subscript	A marking (ͺ) that can appear beneath the vowels α, η and ω, i.e. as ᾳ, ῃ, ῳ. This represents the traces of an original iota sound attached to some words, which eventually became so weak that it was retained only in the spelling.
irregular verb	A verb which does not follow a predictable pattern, e.g. εἰμί, *I am*; οἶδα, *I know*.
linking verb	Examples of linking verbs in Greek include εἰμί, *be*; γίγνομαι, *become*; and φαίνομαι, *seem*. The elements of a clause that are 'linked' by such verbs both appear in the nominative case: e.g. ὁ Σωκράτης ἐστι φιλόσοφος, *Socrates is a philosopher*. In this example ὁ Σωκράτης, *Socrates*, is the subject, whereas φιλόσοφος, *philosopher*, is the complement.
macron	A line placed over a vowel to indicate that it is long (rather than short), e.g. ᾱ, ῑ, ῡ. The macron is an aid to pronunciation typically found only in grammar explanations: you will ***not*** generally find macra in Greek texts and should not reproduce them when writing.
main clause	The principal clause in the sentence and one which (unlike subordinate clauses) would make sense grammatically if it stood alone. In the sentence 'I saw the girl today who(m) I met last week', the clause 'I saw the girl today' is the main clause (and makes sense on its own) whereas 'who(m) I met last week' is the subordinate clause (and does ***not*** make sense on its own).
masculine	One of the three genders of Greek nouns. In vocabulary lists, masculine nouns are distinguished by the definite article ὁ: e.g. ὁ φίλος, *friend*.

middle In Greek, the dictionary form of most middle verbs ends in -ομαι, e.g. ἔρχομαι, *I come/go*; θεάομαι, *I watch*, etc. 'Middle' is one of the three voices in Greek, the others being active and passive. (On the difference between the active and middle forms of verbs, see Appendix Four.)

mood Whether a verb is in the indicative, imperative (or optative). (There is also a fourth mood in Greek, the subjunctive, which is not covered in this module: see *G&E*, pp. 300–4, §274–81.)

negative In Greek, the words οὐ (also spelt οὐκ or οὐχ) and μή are negatives. These allow the expressions of denials, refusals and prohibitions, e.g. οὐ παύει, *he is not stopping*; μὴ παῦε, *don't stop*! οὐ is the more common negative, with μή reserved for special situations – most commonly the negation of an imperative (as in the example: μὴ παῦε, *don't stop*!).

neuter One of the three genders of Greek nouns. In vocabulary lists, neuter nouns are distinguished by the definite article τό: e.g. τὸ ἔργον, *deed.*

nominative The case of the subject of the verb, e.g. τὸν βάρβαρον ὁρᾷ ὁ ναύτης, *the sailor sees the barbarian.*

noun A person, animal, place, thing, event, idea or concept, e.g. ναύτης, *sailor*; ἵππος, *horse*; Ἀθῆναι, *Athens*; νῆσος, *island*; νίκη, *victory*; ὕβρις, *violence, aggression*. In vocabulary lists, nouns are usually listed with a definite article (ὁ, ἡ or τό) to indicate their gender.

number Whether a noun, verb, pronoun or adjective is singular or plural.

object See direct object.

object complement A word or phrase that further describes the (direct) object of a sentence, e.g. καλὸν ποίει τὸν λόγον, *he makes the story beautiful*. The case of object complement is the same as that of the person or thing it describes: i.e. the accusative. An adjective (e.g. καλός-ή-όν, *beautiful*) will also agree with the person or thing it describes (e.g. τὸν λόγον) in number and gender. (Thus καλόν in the example sentence is the accusative singular masculine version of the adjective.)

optative A mood in Greek which is used to express sentiments such as 'would', 'could' and 'might' (it also features in a number of grammatical constructions not covered in this module). See *G&E*, p. 169, §186 and p. 182, §192.

part of speech Whether a word is a verb, noun, pronoun, adjective, adverb, preposition, conjunction, interjection or particle.

particle	Short Greek words which frequently have no direct equivalent in English since they often indicate a tone of voice, gesture or facial expression: e.g. ἆρα, which introduces a question, or γάρ, which generally indicates that an explanation or expansion is being given of a previous point (and is therefore often translated as 'for' or 'because'). See *G&E*, pp. 29–30, §39–43.
participle	An adjective derived from a verb. In English, present participles end in *–ing*, e.g. *being*, *running*, *saying*. Past participles most commonly end in *–ed*, e.g. *watched*, *feared*, *pursued* (although many common verbs in English have irregular past participles: *been*, *run*, *said*, etc.)
passive	When the verb is in the passive voice in Greek, the grammatical subject does not perform the action of the verb but, rather, experiences it: e.g. 'I was hit, 'She is being led away'. As can be seen from these examples, in English, the passive is formed by using the appropriate tense of the verb *to be* in conjunction with a past participle. The passive in Greek is not covered in this module.
person	The form of a verb will differ according to the 'person'. There are three 'persons' in both English and Greek: first person (*I* and *we*); second person (*you*, either singular or plural) and third person (*he*, *she*, *it*; *they*).
personal ending	The ending of a verb, which indicates which 'person' is its subject; e.g. the personal ending -ω (as in παύω) indicates that 'I' is the subject of the verb ('I stop'), whereas the personal ending -ουσι (as in παύουσι) indicates that 'they' is the subject ('they stop').
personal pronoun	*I*, *me*, *you*, *he*, *him*, *she*, *her*, *we*, *us*, *them*, etc.
plural	In the case of nouns, pronouns and adjectives, plural is when more than one person or thing is meant: e.g. τὰ πλοῖα, *the ships* (not 'ship'); ὑμεῖς, *you* plural (as opposed to σύ, *you* singular). In the case of verbs, a plural subject indicates that more than one person or thing is performing the action of the verb, e.g. παύομεν, *we stop* (as opposed to παύω, *I stop*).
possessive adjective	*my, your, his, her, its, our, their*
possessive pronoun	*mine*, *yours*, *his*, *hers*, *its*, *ours*, *theirs*
prefix	A word added to the beginning of another word, usually with the effect of modifying its meaning. The most common kind of prefix are prepositions added to verbs, e.g. ἔρχομαι, *I go*; προσ-έρχομαι, *I go towards, approach*.

preposition A word which accompanies a noun (or a pronoun) to communicate ideas such as the location of the action of a sentence in space or time, e.g. *in, at, among, with, through, from, after, opposite.*

present tense The tense used to indicate that the action of a verb is either happening right now (e.g. 'I am running to school') or regularly happens at the current time (e.g. 'I run to school every day': or 'I do run ...'). In Greek, *I am running*, *I run* and *I do run* are all expressed by the same word: τρέχω.

pronoun A word which (effectively) replaces a noun or a noun phrase: *this*, *that*, *he*, *it*, *we*, *they*. 'Look at the ship, it's enormous!'; 'My parents? They're retired now.'

regular verb A verb which changes according to the same pattern as e.g. παύω, *I stop*.

reflexive pronoun A word referring back to the subject of the sentence, indicating that the subject performed the action on him- or herself. In English, the reflexive pronouns are *myself, yourself, himself, herself, itself, ourselves, yourselves* and *themselves*.

reported speech See indirect statement.

rough breathing See breathing.

sentence A group of words which combine according to grammatical rules to express a statement, question, wish or command. A sentence usually contains at least one verb.

singular In the case of nouns, pronouns and adjectives, 'singular' is when one is meant (as opposed to more than one): e.g. ἐγώ, *I* (as opposed to ἡμεῖς, *we*). In the case of verbs, a singular subject indicates that one rather than more than one person (or thing) is performing the action of the verb, e.g. παύει, *he/she/it stops* (as opposed to παύουσι, *they stop*).

smooth breathing See breathing.

stem The part of a verb, noun or adjective that remains when the endings (and any augments) are removed, e.g. the present stem of παύω is παυ-, and the stem of ἄνθρωπος is ἀνθρωπ-.

subject The person or thing performing the action of the verb in a clause. In Greek, the subject is found in the nominative case.

subject complement See complement.

subordinate clause	A clause which depends for its meaning on another clause (usually the main clause of the sentence) and which would not make sense grammatically if it stood alone. In the sentence 'I was relieved when he walked through the door', 'I was relieved' is the main clause (and *does* make sense as a sentence) whereas 'when he walked through the door' is the subordinate clause (and *does not* make sense as a sentence).
superlative	In English, the form of the adjective that gives it the meaning 'most', or '-est': e.g. *most beautiful, biggest, best.* In Greek, a superlative adjective can be translated in a number of ways: e.g. σοφώτατος, can be translated not only as 'wisest' but also 'extremely wise' or 'very wise'.
syllable	The individual spoken units of a word. In English and Greek the basis of each syllable is a single vowel sound or diphthong (although syllables regularly contain one or more consonant sounds, too). Thus παύομεν has three syllables (παύ-ο-μεν) and φιλοσοφία has five (φιλ-ο-σοφ-ί-α).
syntax	The arrangement of words in sentences following the rules of grammar.
tense	Verbs in English and Greek have tenses, e.g. present, future, imperfect. The tense of the verb indicates *when* the action is performed.
transitive verb	A transitive verb is a verb which takes a direct object, e.g. 'see', 'hit': 'I see the Parthenon', 'I hit the water'.
verb	A word expressing an action, state or condition: τρέχω, *I run*; καθεύδω, *I sleep*; εἰμί, *I am*. In Greek, the dictionary form of most verbs ends in either -ω (παύω) or -ομαι (ἔρχομαι).
vocative	The case used to address someone (or something) directly: ὦ ναῦτα, (*o*) *sailor*!; ὦ πόλι, (*o*) *city*! On uses of the vocative case see Section 3 'Cases and their uses'.
voice	Greek has three voices: the active, middle and passive (which is not covered in this module). On the difference between the active and middle forms of verbs, see Appendix Four.